To Matthew,
I hope you enjoy my story.
[signature] 10/5/14

Keep On Pushing

———————

My Life with a Spinal Cord Injury

———————

By Derek Hawkins

D1280108

© 2010 Derek Hawkins
All Rights Reserved.

No part of this publication may be reproduced, stored in a retrieval system, or transmitted, in any form or by any means, electronic, mechanical,
photocopying, recording, or otherwise, without the written permission of
the author.

First published by Dog Ear Publishing
4010 W. 86th Street, Ste H
Indianapolis, IN 46268
www.dogearpublishing.net

ISBN: 978-160844-577-6

This book is printed on acid-free paper.

Printed in the United States of America

Dedications

So much of my life has changed since that fateful day of my injury in 1984. I could not then have imagined just how far I've come. Yet I realize with undeniable clarity that none of this occurred in a vacuum, that indeed there was a great deal of help along the way. First and foremost have been the strength, hope, and resilience of my Mom and Dad. It is they who deserve all the credit in the world for the person I am today. Not lagging in importance has been the enduring love of my beautiful and caring wife, Heidi. She has always seen beyond the chair, and it was her unwavering support that helped transform this book from a mere idea to a tangible reality. To these individuals I owe so much.

Table of Contents

INTRODUCTION

It seems to me, upon honest reflection, that the idea for providing an account of my life began in congruence with being injured. Ever since being hit by a car as a child I have carried an unrelenting desire to share my experience with others. Over the years, the exact method of doing so was up for much personal debate.

Originally, I contemplated putting my life story to song. Here I encountered two forbidding obstacles. First, I have no great love for the sound of my voice. Second, without an ear for melody I had a difficult time matching a rhythm to lyrics. And even though I still gave it half a chance, songwriting proved far from enjoyable and I ultimately gave it up.

Then in the summer of 2000 I was struck by the urge to express my thoughts and feelings through poetry. Now mind you, I had never before been mistaken for a poet. In all honesty, I wasn't much into reading it either, though to be fair, my mother authored many eloquent poems in her teens and early adulthood that I could certainly appreciate. Still, it was through this aforementioned urge that I discovered an unknown talent for poetry, albeit one that I'd consider raw and needing significant practice for development. Nevertheless, I was able to produce a volume of which, while small, I can still be proud.

Unable to draw enough inspiration to proceed in this genre, my thoughts turned to writing a novel. The storyline would be that of a physically debilitating injury leading a young man through the tumultuous inner journey from anger to acceptance. However, after careful consideration it seemed this avenue led to more work than it would be worth, having to create a world of fictitious characters that manipulated environments and engaged in thought patterns that could more easily be described through the lens of personal experience. So it was that I at last settled on the genre of a memoir.

Among the reasons for writing this book is one that is primarily self serving. It has nothing to do with money, either. (Though if by some chance this work becomes a national best seller and brings with it vast riches, I will surely not turn the money away.) Rather, what makes this a selfish endeavor centers around my own insecurity about one day leaving this earth and eventually being forgotten. The fact that my existence is a mere blip on the radar that is the continuum of time is not of great comfort. After all, using the clock as a reference, it is said that the arrival of the human race coincided within the last minute of a given hour. In those terms it would appear that the average human life span accounts for a mere nanosecond since the dawning of our universe.

Granted, I am early enough into my fourth decade that I anticipate having several more years of viable life experience ahead. However, it is difficult to escape the feeling of time progressing faster with increasing age. Much like a runaway train continuing to gather speed, the momentum of time can not be stopped. Becoming more in tune with my own mortality and the fear it provokes about being forgotten, I see the writing of this memoir as a step toward securing for the ages a record of my existence.

I become filled with anxiety when imagining one of my descendants some three hundred years from now constructing a family tree and lacking any information besides my name and perhaps the cause of death. Settling on the realization that I am not bound to achieve worldwide fame or be recognized by the masses, I can at least be comforted in having left behind a tangible account of the life and times of myself, Derek Andrew Hawkins. In fact, it is with great excitement that I think about who in the future might be reading these words I now put to paper.

Perhaps more than anything, I hope this memoir may serve as inspiration for those faced with similar challenges. The passing of time has brought with it a sense of responsibility to give back and help others. I feel it is a grave disservice to withhold information that may help someone else, regardless of the person or their issue. Such sharing is bound to have benefits not only for the recipient, but the messenger as well. The receiver may be comforted in the knowledge they are not alone. This is no small benefit, as the power of connection can act as a ground to the otherwise electrified current of lost hope and despair.

In turn, the therapeutic value of self-disclosure is the personal reinforcement that I am a survivor of my circumstances. Those who see themselves as victims are so selfishly consumed by their own problems that they may desire solutions but not work for them. I refuse to be a victim.

Facing facts, having to live the majority of one's life in a wheelchair is not topping anybody's list of sought-after experiences. Having been dealt these cards, the opportunity to have a worthwhile life is dependent on deciding to make the best of things as they are. And so I have made that choice. I would encourage others to do the same.

For able-bodied readers, perhaps a new respect for the mental toughness of people with disabilities will be gained. In a culture that generally places more value on appearance than character it is difficult, if not impossible, for people with disabilities to effectively navigate the environment without a strong psyche. It is a grave injustice to categorize people through the lens of preconceived prejudices. The way I see it, there is nothing to lose by having an open mind when confronted with the differences among us. At our core is our humanness. There is absolutely no reason why we all can't just get along.

One concern has held me back from embarking on this project earlier. I make my living as a licensed clinical social worker. In the course of performing therapy it is important, at times, to prevent a client from sharing too much in any one session. This is especially true in the beginning of the therapeutic process. Someone may not return if, after leaving the counselor's office, there is a feeling of extreme shame and vulnerability from having let out too much too fast.

As it relates to the writing process, I had to wait until growing comfortable enough in my own skin before putting myself out there for all to witness, a process that took a considerable number of years. After all, for this work to be a true representation of my life there could be no holding back. Previously unprepared to face judgment, in order for my aforementioned goals to be accomplished it is a risk I am now willing to take.

In fact, it is a misapprehension to believe that escape from the judgment of others is even possible. Instead of harboring resentment or shame over this, I am proposing the benefit of letting people in so that they may consider that there really is more than meets the eye. I do this, too, not in hope of soliciting pity or any other type of condescension. That is not what I worked so hard in my life to receive. Rather, it is the hope that people will appreciate the need to check their assumptions and prejudices against the reality that comes from an honest attempt at getting to know a person. As a human being prone to making snap judgments, let me be the first to admit this is not an entirely easy practice.

As a final statement, I would like to share that in my profession I have come across many individuals society tends to shun. These include, but are not limited to, the working poor and homeless. Yet having the opportunity to interview one of these folks never ceases to produce some startling insights. Having had this experience, I have become extremely sensitive to the certainty that we all come from somewhere and there is a rich history to each and every life. I would venture to say there is none among us who does not have an interesting story to tell. And so there exists a tremendous opportunity to learn from one another in such a way. All it takes is to open up and listen to ourselves and others. In this context, I look forward to sharing my own story in the following pages.

CHAPTER ONE

B. C.
(Before Collision)

I'm excited. *Thoroughly* excited. I am eight years old, and my world is about to expand beyond the confines of the neighborhood streets I have become accustomed to exploring. Bored of exploring is more like it. Protective as they are over their lone offspring, my parents keep a keen tab on my whereabouts and don't afford me the opportunity of straying too far from their collective sight.

Sure, I went places as a child. Who didn't? The method of getting from point A to B, though, was invariably accomplished via automobile. Things are seen along the way but not actually experienced. You witness the dog but not the heavily studded collar around its thick canine neck. A building, seemingly generic in its distant appearance, in fact has one of the most elaborate spider webs attached to its overhang that you will ever see. But alas, in the vehicular mode of travel, this majesty is missed. Time passes too fast when traveling in a car, bus, van, or truck. Sights go by in a blur while the details of the world are lost. Today was going to be different though. Today would allow for greater focus.

I remember playing a sort of game with my mother in which I'd ask permission to ride my bicycle around the block any odd number of revolutions ("Please Mom, can I just go another eleven times?"). She would more than likely say yes, and sure enough I'd be careful to count so as to make sure the agreement was exactly met. Then of course I would go back asking for more.

In hindsight it seems like such a trivial thing, but at the time it was huge. The world seemed so big then. As a child, being able to explore it on your own is nothing short of magical. Having to be accompanied by Mom or Dad as they drive the five minutes to the local 7-11 is as mundane as getting up in the morning. However, riding your bike to the same place can make you feel like Christopher Columbus venturing out and discovering new land. I hated that this was something I had heretofore never been granted permission to do. I thought I would forever be regulated to the increasingly unfulfilling circles around the block. Fortunately, that was not to be the case. Like I said, things were about to change.

It started with an invite from two of my playmates at the time, Johnny and Brian Panzella. They lived in a one floor ranch similar in style to our house and most of the other homes in our neighborhood in Holbrook, New York. I remember vividly the day we first met. I was four years old and we had just moved into our new house. My parents, both just twenty-seven years old, had bought one of the last remaining lots in a new development that featured many other first-time home buyers.

Since the house was built from scratch, my father would take me on occasion to visit the construction site. With each trip there'd be an opportunity to witness additional progress. The lawn, no more than a series of dirt piles at the outset, came to life as if by magic with the application of lush green sod patches. From their skeletal beginnings, the bone-like beams eventually found themselves covered with the less penetrable skin of rooftop, shingles, windows and doors. With its front and back yards on approximately a quarter acre, three bedrooms, single-car garage and full-sized basement, our new home was a sight to behold for a little boy used to residing in an apartment.

At any rate, there I was at the age of four clinging to the leg of my mother or father (it's hard to remember which) on our front lawn while they spoke with the next door neighbors, Tom and Eileen Anderson. As they talked, my attention was drawn to a group of kids around my own age playing in the street directly in front of our property. I suppose sensing my gaze, my parents encouraged me to go down just past the driveway and make friends. Rather nervously, I did as I was told. Once I entered their immediate vicinity, they each looked up to see who this intruder was that had just invaded their space. It's not that they were unfriendly, just that I wasn't greeted with the utmost excitement. When asked for my name, I promptly responded it was "Erik." Not "Derek," but "Erik."

To me it sounded better, a more common name that would help me fit in. I think that's the main reason I grew up having a dislike for my name. It was too different. I wanted a regular name that wouldn't force me to stand out.

I couldn't keep it up, though, feeling too guilty perhaps for this blatant attempt at misdirection. Almost as soon as the words parted my lips I made the correction and let it be known that my name was really "Derek." There wasn't a grand response in return. No formal handshake or exchange of pleasantries. There was only a passive "Hi," and a swift resumption of whatever activity was being enjoyed prior to my intrusion. This constituted my welcome to the neighborhood.

One of the boys, Johnny Panzella was a year older than I, his brother Brian a year younger. Their father was a riot. He would invariably greet us neighborhood kids with the same question, "Does your face hurt?" Whether answered with a "yes" or a "no" there would always be the same response, "Well, it's killing me!" He was one of the really cool dads on the block, one that did not on most occasions convey an air of intimidation or superiority. When he did flex his parental muscle, it was mainly in the form of a very loud and high pitched whistle. Sound was generated by a technique I never could master, the one where you place the thumb and pointer in the corners of your mouth and blow. To this day Mr. Panzella's whistle is the loudest I've ever heard. You never saw two kids run for home so fast as when that siren sounded. It was a sure bet they were about to get in trouble for something.

And so it happened on a warm and bright summer day four years later that I was asked if I'd like to join them to go to the store. Big deal, right? Well, actually it was. This outing was not to be your run of the mill, "Let's hop in the car and do some errands." No, no, no. This was more along the lines of taking advantage of the day to travel the ten or so miles on each of our two-wheeled modes of transportation. This was going to be an adventure of monumental proportions.

Having been invited in the first place was cause for jubilation. Truth be told, at that early age I was not the most popular of the group. My personality at the time can best be described as submissive. I was not comfortable imposing my presence on any type of social situation, even among my peers. Conformity was the key as far as I was concerned, which at times put me teetering on the edge of being an almost complete people-pleaser. Now I don't care who you are, but the latter is downright impossible to achieve on a universal basis, a lesson I was bound to learn the hard way. In this I was schooled rather early on.

Next door to the Panzella's resided Danny Neville, especially popular for having a full-sized above-ground swimming pool. Danny called upon me at age seven to have a specialty item purchased for him in anticipation of his birthday sleep-over party. The gift in question was an inflatable set of biceps that, when flat, could fit under a normal-sized tee shirt. A concealed pump could be operated for simulating a transformation from Bruce Banner into the Incredible HULK. My advance promise to him of making this happen did not come to fruition. As would most kids, I failed to take into account the expense of the item. Needless to say, the puzzle game my mom selected did not go over particularly well.

The vulnerability I was prone to was often taken advantage of. I remember being picked on a lot. I was a tag-along kind of kid in relation to the other neighborhood children. When there was nothing better to do, it became "let's-pick-on-Derek-time." On numerous occasions I was chased down on my bicycle or on foot until reaching the sanctuary of my driveway or another part of our property. What would ensue usually consisted of a back-and-forth name calling process that would deteriorate into repeated bouts of yelling, "I know you are but what am I?" Highly intelligent stuff, let me tell you.

Then there was "ghost riding," an indignity particularly painful to endure. Do you recall this phenomenon? Perhaps this is a universal practice. Just in case though, I will explain further with greater detail. "Ghost riding" consisted of someone taking your bicycle and running beside it while holding on to the seat and handle bars on one side. After gathering a modicum of speed, the bike would be allowed to fly down the street without a rider, thus seeming to be steered by a ghost. Momentum was sure to give way to the laws of gravity, resulting in a crash of some sort amidst the howls and derisive cheers of one's supposed friends.

Looking back, I can appreciate that kids are kids, who at times can be quite mean for no particular reason. To be sure, I was never the brunt of the most abusive treatment. Such behavior was reserved for a few other unfortunate souls. One was Ricky, a.k.a Ricky-Ticky-Tavi. Boy, did he ever hate being called that. He wasn't at all shy about fighting you on it, either. Problem was, Ricky didn't help the situation by the manner in which he fought. Like a girl, pulling the hair of his opponent was a Ricky trademark. For this he was further teased and almost completely ostracized, which makes it surprising that I would ever find myself alone in his house. I did, though, on one afternoon that caused me a heap of trouble. His house being only around the block from ours, I hadn't thought to tell my parents where they could find me. Watching television as we were with Ricky's father, the hour was getting late. Unbeknownst to me, I was being searched for quite diligently. As it turned out, I was in one of the last places my parents would have thought, as Ricky's house was way down on their list of calls. Relieved to find me, they nevertheless subjected me to a stern lecture for the amount of worry I had caused.

Another of the least-liked kids was Chipper, a name often mocked with the moniker of Chips-A-Hoy. Chipper got the worst ribbing in the summertime. Extremely pale skinned, his legs and feet were ghostlike. For this he was laughed at to no end. Eventually Chipper and I became good friends; in fact, his was the longest lasting of all my childhood friendships.

With age, the degree to which I was accepted began to grow. I increasingly became more part of the "in" crowd, to the point that by age nine I had formed what could be considered genuine friendships. My feeling is that such acceptance coincided with a realization that I had a function within the group. Namely, I had developed an ability to play sports at a level on par with the oldest kids on the block. My proficiency especially showed itself when adopting the position of goalie in organized little league soccer and neighborhood street hockey.

The prospect of playing professionally as an adult was a favorite daydream. Of course, back then it didn't seem like a dream as much as just a matter of time before it actually happened. The naïveté of youth, one could say, is truly without limits. Yet even though the signing of a major league contract would not prove to be in the cards for me or any of my childhood playmates, I was nevertheless able to achieve at least one athletic moment in the sun.

It occurred while playing what turned out to be my last season of youth soccer. My father was the coach of our team. Late in the season we were scheduled to play a premier team which, until the point of facing us, had gone undefeated. With substantially less firepower, it was expected we would lose, and by a fairly wide margin. Formulating a brilliant game plan, my dad employed the strategy of putting our best players on defense to help neutralize the other team's potent scoring capabilities. And while it was customary for goalkeepers to alternate positions between halves, I had approached my father and won the opportunity to play the entire game as the last line of defense. In an extremely close contest we ultimately came out on top by a score of 1-0, netting an early goal in transition and holding on for the stunning upset victory. Though I am far from the bragging type, it could not be denied that I played tremendously while making a few particularly difficult game-saving stops. The results were even mentioned in the local town newspaper, with my name among those in print for all to see.

Now getting back to the long bicycle trek made with Johnny, Brian, and Mr. Panzella, the trip itself was overwhelmingly successful, even aside from our safe return. Most of all, it afforded me the tremendous opportunity of establishing a greater bond among my two playmates. Quite fondly, I can recall a lot of laughter and joking along the way, with the ultimate laugh on us as nobody remembered to bring a water bottle! Not to be denied, we soldiered on, experiencing the intoxicating thrill of pedaling along in previously unexplored territory. Without question, this ranked among the most fulfilling experiences of my entire childhood.

CHAPTER TWO

Sudden Impact

It's amazing how fast things can change. A person can appear the picture of health only to suddenly meet their fate with a fatal heart attack. Through no fault of our own, each one of us could be killed or maimed in an instant by a careless motorist. How about an airplane malfunction at 20,000 feet? Take your pick. The fragility of life, while not very often considered, is very real and can be downright scary.

Unfortunately for me, this was to become evident on the afternoon of June 28, 1984. Much unlike its precedent, the second longest bicycle ride I would ever take did not conclude on a similarly positive note. In fact, it came perilously close to resulting in my complete demise.

Shortly following the conclusion of another school year, the day started out well enough, with beautiful summer weather. For me it had been the third grade, and it marked one of the few times I demonstrated some academic difficulties. Reading comprehension was the specific issue, brought to my parents' attention on parent-teacher night. What seemed to do the trick of resolving it was relocating me to a different section of the classroom. Not coincidentally, in the area of the room from which I was removed sat Danny Neville, whose humor could be quite distracting.

On the tenth day of that June month I received a brand new bicycle in celebration of my ninth birthday. A thing of beauty, this bike was. My very first with handlebar breaks, its frame was silver and it had black padded accents. As far as I was concerned, it was the epitome of coolness. Judging from their reactions, my peers tended to agree.

So there I was, faced with the warmth of a late June day and a new ride desperate to be broken in. With these optimal conditions I sought to accompany two of my older friends, Chris and Anthony DiMenna, as they planned to cycle over to a bike shop approximately a half hour's worth of pedaling away. Not particularly thrilled with the idea to begin with, after some degree of nagging, my mom relented in her concern about the lack of adult accompaniment just enough to let me go. The wheels, pardon the pun, had been set in motion.

The trip leading to our destination was entirely uneventful. Having arrived, in my mind's eye I can still see my able-bodied form gawking at a supply of decorative stickers displayed under a glass countertop. One that stood out spelled "Mongoose" in a particularly impressive spotted pattern. I wanted it for my own but was without means for its purchase. Next time, I told myself, next time for sure.

We did not idle there too long. In fact, leaving one moment sooner or later may have been enough to avert the disaster that lay ahead. Peculiar as it may sound, there is *one* thing I distinctly remember from that ride home. Cycling along the shoulder of a fairly main road, at one point I looked down to see a woman's driver's license that had either been lost or discarded. Contemplating for a moment whether or not I should pick it up, I quickly decided not to. Here was an opportunity that would have perhaps changed my waiting destiny for the better.

It all goes blank from there and has remained so ever since. I have no memory of the car, of being hit, nor of the tremendous pain that must have followed. Faced with such an immense trauma, my mind demonstrated its amazing ability to protect itself from that which it could not handle. Essentially, the lights went out. Like an overloaded circuit, my brain completely shut down.

In the end, I had to rely on information provided by family and friends to fill in the blanks about the details of my accident. This was to come many years later. Indeed, it wasn't until the summer of 1998, some fourteen years after, that I gained the whole picture of what had actually happened.

Nevertheless, there was a large part of me that thought I already knew the entire story. In my parents' possession was a copy of the official police report. It stated there had been no direct adult witnesses to the accident besides the lone driver himself, a fifty-five year old Caucasian male operating a Cadillac. With its stretched body and lack of aerodynamics, this was as behemoth a car as you could find in the early to mid 1980's. Proceeding as he was on an otherwise desolate stretch of pavement, the driver's claim was that I recklessly darted into the middle of the road upon maneuvering around the back of a parked van. By the time he saw me, it was too late.

Left with this image, I carried a great deal of guilt for my condition. Such an explanation made me feel that the accident was totally my fault and obscenely preventable. The prevailing self dialogue went along the lines of, *"If only I hadn't been so careless this never would have happened!"* But there was always one detail which never sat right with me: it was initially a hit and run. Granted, the driver did return to the scene shortly thereafter. It begged the question, though, that if the responsibility for the accident was so one-sided, why was there a need to flee? Panic or shock were two possible explanations. Yet as time passed, I couldn't help but think there was something more.

Armed with this growing doubt, I eventually mustered enough resolve during the summer of 1998 to contact my old friend Chris DiMenna. Mind you, this was a person I had not spoken to in ages; we grew apart shortly after I was hurt. Actually it's more apt to say that he distanced himself from me. This bore itself out after I returned home for good following nine grueling months in the hospital. Dreadfully bored and as yet unable to independently leave the house, I called upon him quite often to come over and play. With increasing regularity Chris or his mom would report he was out, going out, or too busy. I eventually got the hint. Reluctantly and with some resentment, I was left feeling the door close on our friendship.

It appeared meant to be when I finally decided to reach out to him again. Calling his parents' home revealed Chris was in the process of moving and would soon be out of state. Having been given a contact number, I rather nervously placed the call and was forced to resist a strong urge to hang up and forget the whole thing. Through perseverance I was able to set up a meeting with him for the following day. It was an unsettling experience in itself just to hear his very adult voice, considering that the last time we spoke he had been 11 years old. I was relieved to hear he was receptive toward reviewing the events that had such a profound impact on both our lives.

He came over at midday. Palpable was the anticipation of his arrival, hanging in the air so that I could concentrate on nothing else. Since it was a weekday with both parents working, I had the house to myself. Appearing as scheduled (there was a confused mixture of trepidation and hope that he wouldn't show), feeble attempts were made at small talk, but it wasn't long before the subject at hand was broached. After all, this was not about rekindling a past friendship. Through no fault of our own, here was a case of too much history lying between two people for that to happen. Nevertheless, I was encouraged to hear that Chris was attending the rather prestigious Duke University. Like me, he appeared to have come through the other side of the tragic event shared between us, though without a doubt there had to exist some extensive emotional scarring. As far as I'm concerned, no human being can go through such an experience totally unscathed. From my perspective it was satisfying to know that what he had witnessed didn't seem to stop him from finding success in life.

What I learned from Chris's account of the accident was nothing short of astounding. He told a very different story from what I had been led to believe. For starters, apparently there was no van that I darted from behind. All three of us together had been in the process of crossing the street. There I was, pedaling along while bringing up the rear of our trio. Having just reached the other side, Chris spotted an oncoming vehicle. He recounted having turned his head around just in time to see the car clip my back tire, sending me flying up over the hood before landing limp some fifteen feet away.

From this meeting I gained much more than the valuable knowledge of what I believe to be the truth of how I became a paraplegic. Seeing the sequence of events through Chris's eyes, I came to appreciate the magnitude of trauma endured by my childhood friend. Moving away from the perspective of being angry with him for having abandoned me, considering what he had witnessed I have no idea how Chris, at so young an age, was strong enough to have maintained any semblance of a relationship with me in the first place.

The events immediately following impact were related primarily through my mom. Statistically speaking, an accident is most likely to occur within a mile or so of a person's home. Such was the case with me. After I was hit, Anthony, the oldest of us, sent his brother Chris to race home and get help. Relying solely on him I never would've made it, punctuating the great fortune I have to be alive to tell this tale.

Just a block over from the road on which I lay was a service truck of the former Long Island Lighting Company (LILCO), now the Long Island Power Authority (LIPA). Apparently servicing some electrical power lines, two workers had heard the crash from their perch and thankfully had rushed over to investigate its source. Upon arrival they happened upon my still and badly injured body, which had stopped breathing. Trained in CPR, they sprang into action and immediately began its application. Amidst the growing chaos an ambulance was summoned.

Meanwhile Chris had reached his house and informed his parents about what had transpired. My mother was then greeted with the worst news of her entire life. She in turn called my father, who had been at work and knew nothing about my venture. While not having any definitive facts about my condition, her maternal instincts had my mom expecting the worst. She recalls having an out of body experience, seeing herself from above like a conscious shadow as her mind attempted to detach itself from a reality it did not wish to face. In this desperate quest for denial we shared a brutal connection.

Escorted by her friend Mary DiMenna, my mother arrived at the scene of the accident only to be overwhelmed by the flurry of activity as my lifeless body was attended to by medical personnel from a recently arrived ambulance. Though dying to get closer, my mom knew she had to let the professionals do their work. It was at that point when, in her periphery, she made out the figure of an older male with a grandfatherly appearance. While not being prepared to do anything about it, she could sense that this was the person responsible for my tenuous condition.

I was finally set to be transported to a local hospital. It was then my mom could tell that nothing would ever be the same again. The projected path of my life had taken a severe turn toward the unexpected and previously unimagined. My mother's heart sank when she saw my legs flopping at the end of the stretcher as I was loaded into the back of the ambulance. She knew in that instant I would never walk again; a moment she sorely wished to be mistaken.

CHAPTER THREE

Starting Over

D uring the trip to the community hospital in Brookhaven I was treated as a celebrity of sorts. The main artery leading to my destination was Route 27, Sunrise Highway, which runs east and west and cuts through most of Long Island. The entire highway was littered with traffic lights at that time, not an ideal situation considering that seconds could literally mean the difference between life and death.

In order to improve these conditions, reinforcements were called upon that resulted in my ambulance benefiting from a police escort. To further help matters, vehicles were prohibited by the authorities from entering along the few miles to be navigated. As I was en route, my father had already left work to meet us at the emergency room. My mom hitched a ride with me.

Upon arrival at Brookhaven Hospital I was rushed to a trauma room where a team of doctors hovered over and began to treat my mangled body. I had a severely broken right leg. From that wound there was internal bleeding which manifested as an obscenely distended abdomen. I remained without any signs of independent respiration and was unresponsive to all outside stimuli. There was also a noticeable bruise on the back of my head. The abrasion raised fears that I had endured significant brain damage, placing me into a permanently vegetative state. I was ruled to be in a coma.

Having made the assessment, the lead physician confronted my parents with the news that they could no longer do anything for me. My future, he posited, was destined to be spent attached to a respirator, with continued absence of brain activity. The upshot was that I should be let go and read my last rites. A priest had already been called upon.

My parents were both understandably shaken to hear this bleak outlook. Unable to accept such news at face value, my father demanded to see me. With that, my parents were led to my side. What they witnessed had to be far removed from what could have ever seemed possible just a few short hours before. Seeking some sort of response, my dad started to call my name. There was no reaction.

For whatever reason, he did not stop. With each attempt he became sterner in tone. Still there was nothing, and yet to this day my father insists he knew I was in there. Emotions running high as they were, he made the most desperate effort to get my attention by loudly ordering me to open my eyes. Something miraculous then occurred, of which I have no memory. I looked straight at him.

Such a death-defying act brought a flurry of activity. To their credit, the medical personnel quickly determined I was in need of much more intensive treatment than could be provided at my current location. My sign of life was accompanied by a transfer to Stony Brook University Hospital. It would have been extremely difficult, if not impossible, on that day for anyone to predict I would graduate, as I did, from the state college of the same name located on the opposite side of the road.

With my arrival to the emergency room some twenty minutes later, the first order of business was rushing me into surgery. At the operating table, the main highlights included the doctor's ability to set my fractured femur and stop my internal bleeding. It took several hours for them to finish. After a stint in the recovery room I was placed on the pediatric intensive care unit. This became my home for the next three months.

My mom recounts the story of when I first woke up, some twelve hours or so after the initial trauma. I do not recall any of this, but she says that my eyes opened with an expression of fear and sadness. A tear formed at the corner of my eye and fell to the pillow. Alone with me in the private hospital room, my mother was quick to identify my whereabouts and put my mind at ease as much as possible. Almost immediately, I was fast asleep.

I must have been some sight to behold, one that only a mother could love, so to speak. I was engulfed in tubes and life preserving hardware, even the act of breathing itself done for me by a respirator. My right leg was suspended in midair, bent at the knee in traction. Pins were inserted through the leg at strategic points to help the bones stay together and heal properly.

Furthermore, having suffered a collapsed right lung, I was fitted with a tracheotomy tube. Like the promise of a new day, losing the lung was a given if not sufficiently drained of excess fluid. Being dreadfully weak and immobile, there were no expectations of me doing this on my own. Instead, the suctioning of fluid would be accomplished by regularly inserting a catheter through the short tube jutting from the front of my neck. In this way my dust bunnies of phlegm were removed. Topping off this pathetic image, a bolt had been fixed in my skull to help measure cranial pressure and decipher to what extent brain damage had occurred. To be fair, in this regard the question on the doctors' minds wasn't so much whether, but how much.

It is difficult to pinpoint the first thing I remember after the accident. What comes to mind are some of the dreams I had. I venture to say that these occurred during the limited time I spent in a coma, though of this I cannot be certain. In the first dream I was Popeye the Sailorman, a character from one of my favorite movies and cartoons in childhood. A year or so prior, I had seen the film, which starred a very young funnyman named Robin

Williams. On the same night I returned home and fashioned myself as Popeye, practicing cartwheels in my bedroom with a toy pipe firmly planted in the corner of my mouth.

As Popeye in my dream, I was at the bottom of a downward moving escalator. At the top was the menacing form of Bluto, who had one arm wrapped around the waist of a screaming Olive Oyl. She was repeatedly imploring me to help her. The problem was that I found myself hunched over on all fours in a much weakened state. What made matters worse was that in Bluto's other hand was what I needed most to heed my captured love's call, that all-important can of spinach. And so there my nemesis remained, mocking me from above as I watched helplessly while growing weaker and weaker with each moment.

My other dream found me in just as precarious a situation. In it I was walking through a vast parking lot filled with a varied selection of automobiles. At some point I attempted to walk sideways between a pair of cars that were parked facing one another, their front bumpers almost touching. Halfway through I became hopelessly stuck. In my struggles to break free I ended up wedging myself in even tighter, seemingly ending any opportunity for escape. Added to this troublesome situation was that from my vantage point I spotted a collection of G.I. Joe action figures lying just beyond my reach. As a youth, these were by far my favorite toys. I spent hours of play time setting up and reenacting a wide range of battle sequences between the forces of good and evil. To be so close to reaching a plethora of these characters was pure agony. Of particular note in this dream was the absence of any other human beings.

Now as far as dream interpretation is concerned, there is one particular theory of which I am especially fond. It was espoused by none other than the staunchest advocate of psychoanalysis, Dr. Sigmund Freud. The way he understood them, dreams can be divided into two categories, representing either extreme fears or desires. I believe my dreams encapsulated both of these polar opposites. There were incentives in each of them that made me want to do nothing more than press forward. However, fear that this would not be possible soon set in. It was as if my mind, in the only way it knew how, was attempting to come to terms with the newfound limitations of my post-accident condition.

In truth, nobody knew for sure the exact extent of my injuries. Even the doctors could not speak with any certainty. There was very much a "wait and see" attitude among all concerned. To be sure, I was beginning my recovery with a completely blank slate. Like an elevator on the most subterranean floor, the only direction to go was up.

Progress was extremely slow, yet steadily I made gains. Illustrative of the saying you have to start somewhere, the first muscles I gained control over were my eyelids. It was through blinking alone that I was able to communicate with and manipulate my environment (or more accurately, have the environment manipulated for me). In response to questions from family members and medical staff, one blink meant "yes" and two blinks meant "no." In their efforts to determine my level of cognitive function I was quizzed quite often. There was considerable pressure to respond with the correct sequence of blinks. Unfortunately, eyelids can flutter without warning, causing an accidental denial to the slam dunk question of "Are the New York Rangers your favorite hockey team?" At such times suspicions of brain damage would unnecessarily gain momentum.

Eventually the ability to move my head, arms, and hands returned, though in a much weakened state. Turning my head was in itself a major ordeal. It seemed that with each day I was able to rotate my neck just another inch or so. The pain was at times tremendous from my head being stuck in one position for so long. Parallel to my bed as it was, weeks went by before I could look out the window. By that time I had mastered every detail of the pock marked tiles lining the room's ceiling.

When movement returned to my hands there was an almost complete absence of coordination. In order to regain dexterity I was told to attempt touching my thumb to each fingertip of my left and right hands respectively. As simple as it seems to me now, this was a particularly daunting exercise that took months to accomplish fully. In fact, as a means of gaining some perspective during what I might now consider a bad day, performing this task is usually more than enough incentive to snap out of whatever doldrums I may be experiencing.

Regarding my physical awakening, this was where the gains appeared to end, seeming to confirm the doctor's growing opinion that I had a spinal cord injury that rendered me paralyzed from the chest down. Compared with my initial experience of total body paralysis, this was an obvious improvement. Each day, for a measurement tool, the sharp end of a safety pin was lightly scraped along my skin and I would have to respond when the prickling sensation ended, all the while having my eyes closed. No matter how hard I concentrated or tried to convince myself otherwise, the extent to which I could feel my body never reached below the nipple line.

Just a short time after, there was one false alarm that gave everyone some hope that my condition *would* keep improving. One morning at some six to eight weeks A. D. (after disability), my parents arrived at the hospital to learn I had just been able to move my left foot. I remember their excitement at the prospect of me further defying the odds and making a more complete recovery than was expected. Ultimately, it was not meant to be, because what was originally cast as an increase in motor function was just the onset of involuntary muscle spasms. Every day since then, I've relied on the medication Baclofen to help control these otherwise incessant tremors of my lower limbs.

However fleeting, the hope of regaining the use of my legs has to be considered the "high" point of my early hospitalization. To be fair, there was also an unmistakable low when I became convinced I would never be leaving the hospital. Escaping the machines that helped keep me alive appeared too overwhelming. It was a major production just to be led out onto the hospital grounds for a little sunshine. A team effort was required between my parents and nurses to do all the work in making even this simple want possible. With this realization I began to withdraw and shut down. I refused to be brought outside and grew highly resistant to having a shirt put on me. Resigning myself to a life spent within the confines of a hospital, I figured there was no point living a charade of conformity to rules of the outside world.

Finally I reached a point when I requested pictures of the house and bedroom I feared my own eyes would never gaze upon again. This proved too much for my parents to take. While fulfilling my request, in what would become a common theme, they provided words of motivation and encouragement that helped me strive toward overcoming the obstacles that lay ahead. In this case, assurances were made that my room was getting a complete makeover. The provision of such an investment helped me think that somehow, someway, I was going to make it home. I just *had* to experience my new room!

Occurring around the same time, another poignant example comes to mind of the early support provided by my parents. My father had eventually returned to his full time job as a mechanic at Entenmann's Bakery and was at work when I expressed concern to my mom that I would never be able to accomplish certain milestones such as learning to drive a car. Sensing the importance of that moment, and the potential of having me fall into a depression I could ill afford, my mom called my dad at work. He left for the hospital in the middle of his shift to help engage me in a family meeting of sorts. Huddled in close quarters on my bed, they explained that with certain adaptations I would be able to participate in all the activities of my peers which I otherwise would have done if the accident hadn't occurred. This was something I had not previously considered.

I sincerely believe that this impromptu conference was a turning point in my determination to participate diligently in my own recovery. Though I could not verbalize it so succinctly at the time, it was a relief not to waste undue mental energy consumed with worry that I was alone in this process. All I had to do was heed the words of my parents and everything would work out. I chose to do so unconditionally, and I am glad for it.

In fact, I believe I get more credit for my recovery than I actually deserve. For those I hold close and who are privy to all I have been through, there is invariably a sense of wonderment that I was able to persevere at such a young age and get where I am today. On countless occasions I've been approached with the conviction that if put in the same situation at only nine years old, an overwhelming majority of people would not have been so strong.

I'm not so convinced. The way I see it, I am here today not in spite of, but because of the fact I was so young. At that stage of my life I didn't know any better than to listen to my elders and trust in what they were saying to me. If hurt later in life I would've been hard pressed to hold the same innocent view of how the world works. As yet, I was still under the impression that my parents knew everything in the world, and that whatever they said must be true. This viewpoint was instrumental in my ability to trust their assurances. Like any child, I had an intense desire to please my parents. If they determined it was imperative for me to do something, I was going to give it my all, and then some.

Despite my predicament, at the bottom of it all I was still a kid. One truism about children, and I think young boys especially, is that there is a tendency toward mischief. It would seem almost innate, this behavior of continuously testing the boundaries of adult patience. Even in my significantly damaged state I was no different.

Of course, it took a bit of resourcefulness in conjuring an outlet to express myself. Identifying the target of my mischief was the first order of business. I chose the nurses responsible for my care. As far as the means, anyone who has spent time in the hospital or has watched enough television should be familiar with the call button, a splendid device utilized by a patient to indicate the need for assistance in a timely manner. Thinking myself wise with a devilishly funny ploy, my bright idea to abuse this privilege had unintended negative consequences.

Now it ought to be emphasized that in many ways the call button was my lifeline. This was especially true considering the rapid rate at which my lungs could fill with phlegm. At those times I could not wait patiently for the next scheduled suctioning to occur. This was a non-issue during daytime hours when I hardly ever had to give the procedure a second thought. My room was seemingly always occupied during that time by a family member who could summon assistance at a moment's notice. My parents were even trained in how to operate the machinery.

It was a different situation at night with my visitors dwindling toward home for the evening, inevitably leaving me at the mercy of the nurse's availability. Though as darkness accumulated and concern for parental reproach diminished precipitously, with the push of a button I began playing the game of falsely lighting up the "help needed" signal above my hospital room door. With every response to my illuminated door light I would pretend to be sleeping. As I recall, this went on for a couple of hours. I figured (quite erroneously, as it turned out) that each nurse had nothing better to do than indulge me in such behavior.

Like the boy who cried wolf, the time eventually came when I was in dire need of assistance. Having either caught on to my antics or figuring the buzzer was broken, no one responded as readily to check up on me. Incapable of a productive cough, the situation got so bad that I thought I was going to drown to death in my own phlegm. What a terrible way to go! I can see the headlines now: Courageous Boy Survives Car Crash, Done in by Pesky Mucous. Yet just when I thought I wouldn't last any longer, my savior in white came and provided some much needed relief, allowing me to breath normally again. From that harrowing experience I learned my lesson and did not put myself at such risk again.

I would be remiss not to comment on the great deal of gratitude I have for the acts of kindness extended toward me by members of the nursing staff. One of them, Sue Finnigan, worked the early shift and could be counted on for a warm greeting each morning. She carried with her an air of cheer and optimism. Also a good role model for health consciousness, she was pregnant at the time and would often be seen with a carton of milk in her hand, a straw protruding for her drinking convenience. Sue was very much a motherly figure with whom my parents and I quickly bonded. It was Sue that I called upon to do me the favor of purchasing an anniversary present for my folks, celebrated annually on August 25.

By that time my mode of communication had progressed to lip synching and writing, the latter when my mechanical bed was placed in an upright position. The trachea tube made it impossible to talk with a normal voice. I never would master plugging the hole with my finger, creating sound that is altogether synthetic and more resembles a robot voice than anything a human being would naturally produce.

Regarding my parents' gift, I was specific in my request, desiring Sue to purchase the handheld video game version of Donkey Kong. Not exactly on their wish list, I'm sure. Primitive by today's standards, the game took the exact shape of a miniature arcade. What gave me the idea is that they had just bought me something similar, a game with those most famous of brotherly characters, Mario and Luigi, which served the dual benefit of providing me with hours of fun and helping improve my fine motor skills. Having a limited reference as to what they would actually enjoy as an anniversary present, I guess this was also my way of saying thank you.

I encouraged Sue to use the allowance money that my parents had continued to give me on a weekly basis, kept in my hospital room for me to see accumulate. I'm sure she didn't use any of it; that's just the type of person she was. My parents were extremely touched upon receipt of my gift. They were even more amazed that I'd concern myself so much with their anniversary. To my delight, Mom and Dad volunteered to let me play with their gift as much as I liked. I don't think I was ever without it.

Sue was also responsible for setting up one of the greatest thrills of my life. It turned out that she had a connection to Steve Vickers, a former member of the New York Rangers. Knowing that the Rangers were my favorite sports team of all time, she was able to utilize this relationship to my benefit, so that one day Steve Vickers visited me in the hospital. He brought with him myriad official items, including autographed hockey sticks personally signed by individual players and the entire team, player photos, and an official trainer's jacket. It was awesome. I was even named an official member of the alumni association and had articles written about me in their newsletter. Also, it just so happened that this former Ranger great had recently shot a commercial with Wayne Gretzky for the Canon camera company. To my total disbelief, I was given the same stick The Great One used in the commercial. The best player in the history of the sport signed it with best wishes to me on the blade. Yes, I still have it. No, I will never sell it.

As if this wasn't enough, I was cordially invited - with complimentary tickets - to my choice of a home game at the world's most famous arena. It would be the first game I ever attended. Part of this unbelievably generous package included the opportunity to go into the locker room and meet my childhood heroes following the contest. Of course, I wanted to go as soon as possible. However, it was agreed to put it off until spring so that I could work on getting better.

So it was that on April 25, 1985 I saw my team battle their biggest rivals, the New York Islanders. The Rangers got their brains beat in, not surprisingly since the Islanders ruled the hockey world at that time. To me it didn't matter though. Midway through the third period I even got to pick the player of the game, which was subsequently announced over the Madison Square Garden loudspeaker for all to hear. I chose my favorite goal-tender, Glen Hanlon, never mind the fact he let in six goals that night.

Going into the locker room with my dad was a surreal experience. Mom couldn't follow due to player nakedness, of which there was plenty. In fact at one point I found myself seated right next to long-time defenseman Ron Greschner, who was smoking a cigarette with nothing but his socks on. I also remember seeing sharp-shooting forward Pierre LaRouche worked over by trainers, getting treatment for his ailing back. Among other players of note, I also met John Vanbiesbrouk, eventually one of the franchise's most successful goalies but only a rookie on that squad.

Like a kid in a candy store, I didn't want the night to end. My universe had been filled with magic, but there was still something missing since I had not met my idol. Little did I know I was being set up, for just as I thought it was never going to happen, I was approached from behind by someone who put their hands over my eyes. When I turned around he was there before me, Glen Hanlon. In a world where it now seems most athletes are detached from their fan base, seeing his smiling face and genuine eyes made it well worth the wait. To confirm his strength of character, I would months later receive a personal letter of thanks for selecting him as player of the game. My vote so late in the season allowed him to become the team's player of the year. In the letter he wrote, "Maybe next year we will win the Stanley Cup." So what that he was only eight years off the mark and long since retired when that finally happened!

***

While at Stony Brook Hospital there was one other nurse, Rose Mary, with whom I developed a close bond.

She was a young, attractive Italian woman with a slim figure, dark complexion and brown eyes. She wore her black hair big, as was characteristic of the 1980's style. With apologies to Mom, she was the most beautiful woman I had ever seen, and it's safe to say I had a major crush on her. Blessed with an outgoing personality that was easy to engage, Rose Mary made you feel you were among friends.

She worked primarily in the evening and was instrumental in helping me fall asleep. Sleep was hard to come by and at times restricted to a few short hours. For starters, I was perpetually uncomfortable. Not surprising, since spending the majority of three months in bed is bound to get to anyone. There was also a catch-22 in that while I was in need of rest to endure the procedures that lay ahead, it was the anticipation of these inevitably painful treatments that kept me up at night. Desperate for this to change, my parents began instructing the nurses to limit the amount of television I was exposed to at night.

In the end though, it was Rose Mary who did the trick. As a sleep aide she would invariably take some time out of her shift to sit with me. Armed with a great imagination, she would create elaborate stories involving me and my neighborhood friends. Sometimes she would also include my dog Sandy, just about the best friend any boy could have. (She was put to sleep over a decade ago now, but I still carry a picture in my wallet of the greatest pup in the whole wide world). Within these stories Rose Mary would create for me an alternative universe in which I was sent with my companions on amazing adventures. One in particular had us traveling on a safari in search of lost treasure. The environment would be described with such detail that it seemed real. Providing my mind with an outlet to wander towards was a truly invaluable service. Devoid of worry, I'd drift off without fail.

As the dust began to settle and I became a bit more stable, a final diagnosis was supplied. The doctors labeled me a quadriplegic with a complete spinal cord injury (meaning the loss of both movement and feeling) at the C7 vertebra. I'd never walk again and would depend on a wheelchair for the rest of my life.

These latter two prognostications have proven dead accurate, though I have been known to quip on occasion that I've really been faking it all these years. As quite an anomaly, however, I actually have movement to T1 (two vertebrae down from C7). While only a short distance away, the impact on function is huge. Able to consider myself a paraplegic, I have full muscular use of my arms and hands. In the technical sense though, I am still a "quad." The tell-tale characteristic of all four limbs being affected shows itself in certain "dead spots" on my upper extremities. The undersides of both arms, between the elbow and armpit, are totally without sensation.

In layman's terms (quite frankly these are the only terms I myself completely understand when it comes to most medical jargon), the main contributor to the loss of function characteristic of a spinal cord injury is the swelling that accompanies the initial trauma. Like a car dry of oil, without continued blood flow to the affected area, the nerves attached to the cord can not remain viable.

Throughout a great deal of my post-injury life I've felt enormous shame over not being able to feel more than seventy five percent of my body. In a culture that places such extreme value on sex and physicality, my personal shortcomings in these areas were always something I tried desperately to keep hidden.

Furthermore, there had for years been resentment at the extent of my injury, given the harm-reducing medications that have subsequently become available. For instance, if injected into the spinal cord within 24 hours of being injured, a drug called Sygen can significantly reduce the swelling around the cord so that the loss of function is not nearly as great. I struggled mightily with feelings of anger for not being hurt at the "right" time.

Today I do my best to choose a different tack, one that has become easier with age and the increase in self esteem that results from accomplishing life goals. Namely, I bring myself back to those early moments in the hospital when my survival was very much in doubt. I reframe my thoughts to consider how I really am living on borrowed time. When able to get a firm hold on this point of view, the fact that I can't feel my penis doesn't seem like the end of the world.

What also needs to be considered is that technology had evolved enough by 1984 to allow for the possibility of living through my injury. This was not always the case. Historically it was not uncommon that trauma to the spinal cord brought with it a death sentence. It is this ability to look at situations from multiple perspectives that I believe is the key to mental toughness.

CHAPTER FOUR

City Bound

As September approached, I entered my third month in the Intensive Care Unit. There brewed a dilemma of sorts in that my functioning had improved to the point that a transfer out of the ICU was warranted. For one, I gained the ability to tolerate sitting in a wheelchair for extended periods of time. I was also able to perform a certain number of activities of daily living that included feeding myself and brushing my teeth and hair. That said, there was a great deal of hesitation in allowing me to go home. I was still in need of extensive physical therapy, as I did not yet have the strength to push my chair. There was also a need to relearn such activities as dressing and bathing myself. Another matter was that I still had a tracheotomy that required suctioning. Coming home with a hole in my neck was less than optimal.

Thus it turned out that Stony Brook wasn't to be my last extended hospital stay. The option that began to make the most sense among those involved in the decision making process (of which I was not one), was to have me transferred to a rehabilitation hospital. Once deliberated, arrangements were made for me to begin the long rehab process at RUSK Institute, a division of New York University Hospital. On September 18, 1984 I was transported by ambulance from the slower paced suburban lifestyle of eastern Long Island to the frenetic pace that characterized my destination of downtown Manhattan.

Despite just some sixty miles distance within the same state, the difference between a neighborhood street on Long Island and a New York City block is night and day. Like a most spectacular lightning storm, the frenzy of activity associated with the latter beats any other environment. Energy generated by the congestion of cars and people, along with the ricochet of sounds through rows of daunting skyscrapers, is palpable. By contrast, the open space of suburban Long Island landscapes lends itself to a more relaxing atmosphere.

My dad relates having cried a great deal of the way as he followed behind the ambulance during the hour plus trip into good old NYC. This was to be the furthest I had ever been from home. It was upsetting to consider I wouldn't be able to see my parents as often, especially being in a place new and scary to all of us. As it was, they were even able to work this out. Mom ended up taking the train to visit me every day. Being a stay-at-home care-giver, she was able to do so without dancing around an employment schedule. My dad would come on his days off.

And though they by far led the way, my parents were not alone in the provision of a support system. Among the most regular visitors at each hospital were both sets of grandparents. More on the periphery, but still making themselves present, were a number of aunts and uncles. No matter who it was, the greeting I received always began with a smile, each visit generally upbeat in nature. Apparently these were the rules set down firmly by my father and were non- negotiable. There would be no crying or other such demonstration of sadness allowed at my bedside. The world's most renowned psy-chologist could not have suggested a more perfect inter-vention. This standard expectation of positive energy fostered an environment for recovery and healing.

Upon my arrival at RUSK I was made to wait in the lobby for what seemed like hours as the details of my admission were finalized with administration. From a prone position I was unable to effectively decipher my new surroundings. Waves of anxiety swept over me as I

lay upon the ambulance-provided stretcher. My accommodations and amenities finally settled upon, I was
brought to the floor where I'd spend the majority of the
next six months.

The floor itself was quite large. It consisted of two
children's wards, each across the hall from the other and
separated by gender. Each ward was a large room with a
half dozen beds arranged in a semi circle. As one entered
the boy's side, my bed was the first on the right. Exiting
to the left, perhaps fifty to one hundred feet past the
wards were the physical and occupational therapy
departments. Situated halfway in between was the recreation therapy office. Moving some twenty feet in the
opposite direction of the children's wards revealed the
nurses' station. Directly opposite was a spacious community room that served as the main play area and dining
room. At the other end of the hallway was a ward for
adolescents.

What every patient had in common was some type
of physical injury that required therapy to overcome.
There were a few among us who had some very interesting stories. One patient in particular, an older adolescent,
was recovering from a gunshot wound to the back. He
had been left for dead on a high rise metropolitan
rooftop. It was by sheer chance that he had been discovered before dying. By far, the patient with whom I
became most friendly was a girl named Tricia Pikul. With
flowing blond hair and perfect dimples, Tricia was a
beautiful young teenager severely affected by a traumatic
brain injury. Here too I developed a major crush.

Smart as a whip, her injury showed itself mostly
through contracted limbs that forced her to use a wheelchair. Furthermore, the affected area of her brain caused
an inability to effectively manipulate language for communication. When attempting to speak Tricia uttered

mostly indistinguishable sounds. Perhaps more than any-one else besides her own family, by spending a lot of time around her I was able to decipher many of Tricia's wants and needs.

Hers was a sad story; not that any story ending with debilitating injuries is ever a happy one. It began as Tricia and her older sister were going out with their mother. Prior to leaving they got into a bitter argument about who was going to sit in the front passenger seat versus who would be relegated to sit alone in the back of the car. After much debate, Tricia "won" and got to sit up front. In a most horrific example of being careful what you wish for, Tricia's reward was to be hurt much worse than anyone else as her part of the family car took the brunt impact from another fast moving vehicle. It's amazing, really, how such a thing as riding shotgun can instantly go from appearing the most important thing in the world to the most trivial argument of all time.

In no uncertain terms, it would seem a real defect of the human intellect, this severe lack of acute awareness regarding the fragility of life. At times guilty of this myself, too much negative energy is devoted to issues of status that just don't matter. Perhaps naïve in this view-point, I'd nevertheless like to believe there'd be at least half as many arguments between people if we were more in touch with the limits of our collective mortality.

Initially, my nights at RUSK were spent alone in the community room. Unlike at Stony Brook, I wasn't within easy view of my regular sleeping quarters. Given my con-tinued need for lung suction, it was important to remain in close proximity to the nurses' station. It was also con-siderate toward other patients on the ward not to be awoken by the performance of this procedure.

The goal was always to remove my tracheotomy as soon as possible. Having been mostly cleared of congestion,

I was no longer in danger of losing a lung. Therefore it had become time for me to do the work in removing any residual buildup of phlegm. Trouble was, I had become so psychologically dependent on having this done for me that I was convinced that, if removed, I would not survive. In their attempts to wean me from its usage, my parents and the entire medical staff were committed to limiting the number of times they would fulfill my request for suctioning.

Being that there was no call button in the community room, my way of getting the nurse's attention was to ring a miniature version of the Liberty Bell, given as a gift from I don't remember who. The perceived need to have my lungs constantly cleared, along with feeling vulnerable in my new surroundings, had me signaling for assistance at intervals of short duration. Unfortunately, I awoke on one particular occasion in a panic as my bell would not ring. When I was attended to some time later, a laugh was had at my expense with a comment made that the inner piece had been removed purposely.

For the longest time I held a great deal of resentment over this incident. Looking back, though, I believe this was the start of a very valuable lesson. No matter who they are, never should a person feel a sense of entitlement that their needs are required to be met when they say so. I, however, had begun to fall into that line of thinking. With so much attention having been paid to me since the accident, it was a role in which I had become too comfortable. Go figure, but I wasn't the center of the universe after all.

Within a month after my admission, the tracheotomy finally did come out. The occasion of its removal was perhaps the most uncomfortable moment of my life. Removed rather unceremoniously by a doctor at my bedside, there was a feeling of not being able to breathe as the flow of air passed entirely through my neck. Swallowing was a trip as the saliva went no further than back out of the gaping hole. These things did not occur previously as the inserted end of the tracheotomy had a tube that pointed down into the esophagus. A gauze pad was then secured, serving as a temporary membrane that made the job of breathing a bit easier. This dressing would remain in place for a few weeks while the hole had an opportunity to close on its own. The skin that eventually formed remained tender for many years. In fact, significant bouts of coughing caused the area to tingle, making me believe with severe trepidation that the wound was going to reopen. Thankfully it never did.

Another of my most harrowing moments experienced at RUSK might seem quite innocuous to the average person. The event in question had nothing to do with a surgery, lengthy needle, or any other type of painful procedure. Instead, it was the rather benign-sounding task of having an x-ray taken of my back.

In order for the doctors to obtain the desired picture, I had to sit on the edge of a cold, hard x-ray table with my legs hanging over the side. At this stage of my recovery I could not manage to hold that position on my own, much less get there in the first place. I relied almost totally on others for body positioning and balance, and if let go, was basically guaranteed a fall. However, even without being let go, there would invariably be a sensation of falling unless I could both see and feel the person that held on to me. As it was, to accommodate the x-ray machine on this particular occasion, neither condition could be met. Instead, my father was only permitted to support my body from behind, with his hands no farther up than my torso.

This posed a huge problem for me. Not only could I not see the person I was dependent on, I also could not feel him. As clear as day I can recall dear old Dad growing impatient with my endless expressions of fear despite his assurances of never letting me fall. What he did not understand was that the Almighty himself could not have convinced me that I was safe from harm. Holding me as he was, below my line of sensation and not within my line of sight, my dad from this perspective might as well have not been there at all. I felt doomed to crack my head open on the tiled hospital floor. Luckily (and it *was* luck in my mind), that did not happen. The x-ray was taken and I was lifted back into my wheelchair, back to the safety of an environment I could manage somewhat independently. With its high solid back and industrial armrests, a degree of control and security was gratefully restored.

Having the trachea become history brought two undeniably positive consequences. Of major significance was that, with my neck healing, I had regained the ability to talk. After three plus months of being unable to utter a single word, this was a welcome change. Lip synching, while having served its purpose, had proven to be an unreliable means of effective communication. Frustration often ensued for me and the interpretive party as I attempted to get my point across. Especially laborious was having to spell out the words of complete phrases. At times I gave up trying to express my wants and needs.

The other substantial benefit of being trachea-free was the opportunity to go home. Not for good, mind you, but for a weekend. Nevertheless, despite the short duration this was a dream come true.

That opening weekend in November of '84 marked the first time I had been home since the accident. The occasion was not lost on the old neighborhood. Consecrating the special nature of this event, I was treated to a hero's welcome. An array of balloons was strung to our mailbox and a WELCOME HOME DEREK! banner hung over the single car garage. A number of baked goods and other food trays were hand-delivered from neighboring houses. And undoubtedly at the behest of their respective parents, my very young and able- bodied playmates stopped over for abbreviated visits.

As the Saturday afternoon rolled along and the flow of visitors slowed to a mere drip, as if with the coldest wind I was slapped with the reality that **everything** had changed. Granted, my parents had prepared as much as possible. Thankfully, our next door neighbor voluntarily constructed a ramp with an attached deck built upon the front stoop. This allowed for much easier access into our one-story ranch. Work had also begun on my bedroom to make it more accessible. Plans were made to knock down the wall dividing my room and the den so that I would have more space to maneuver. Unfortunately, at the time of my initial visit this indoor renovation was not yet completed.

Further complicating matters was that my chair could not fit into our bathroom. Although the bathroom was eventually gutted and rebuilt for my convenience, at that time to bathe meant having to be carried and placed down into the tub. Performing numbers one and two was a totally different matter, as I did not necessarily have to enter the bathroom for either. For peeing, I relied on an external latex catheter that rolled down to the base of Mr. Winky much like a condom. In order to prevent leaks it was secured there by an adhesive spray. On the tip end was a short rubber tube attached to a drainage bag. Concealed underneath my clothing, the bag had straps that wrapped around either leg and helped keep it in place. When the bag became filled with urine it was emptied into a urinal by lifting my pants leg and turning a valve at its lower end. Forgetting to tighten it back was a rare and unfortunate occurrence resulting in a wet pant leg and sock.

Regarding my bowels, they have been regulated then and since through a bowel program. This consists of inserting a suppository or enema into what my father was known to call the "brown freeway," a. k. a. the rectum, once every other day. While hospitalized it was commonly done in bed, lying on my side with a pad underneath my bottom. Now I can manage with complete independence by utilizing a commode that doubles as a shower bench. Injecting some humor into this practice, a fellow patient referred to his bowel program as a "two sixteen," constituting the numeric position of the letters b and p in the alphabet. Formed on the same premise, I choose to refer to these as my "s and s" ("shit and shower") days. Let's face it, sometimes you have to laugh to save from crying.

My first night home was very uncomfortable. Without my own bed to sleep on yet, I was forced to try my luck in Mom and Dad's waterbed. This only made matters worse when it came to difficulties keeping my balance. What's more, I had become used to hospital beds that could be adjusted to sleep on an angle. Try as they might, my parents could not make me comfortable with pillows propping me up, so that for most of the night I lay awake. At 5:30 a.m. I was allowed to start watching cartoons on the thirteen inch black and white television in my parent's room, the same cartoons that not so long prior, and yet a lifetime away, I enjoyed with the innocent laugh of childhood.

Beyond any doubt, I was scarred by this experience. So much so, in fact, that to my parent's consternation I was quick to turn down my next scheduled weekend at home. They may have been concerned it was a sign that I'd given up. Truth was, I remember being highly conflicted. On one hand, I wanted desperately to be home. At the same time I was more comfortable in the familiar confines of the hospital.

This dilemma would eventually work itself out. In short order my bedroom was completed, with furnishings that included a standard issue hospital bed with full mechanical capabilities. Attached to the bed was a trapeze overhang that allowed for easier position changes and the means for some much needed exercise.

Meanwhile, a central part of my rehabilitation included intensive physical and occupational therapy. As I mentioned before, I had to relearn how to perform the simplest of tasks. As an example, it wasn't until the middle of January that I was able to put on a tee shirt without assistance. The next day I was extremely upset by failing to duplicate my previous success. This demonstrated an emerging characteristic of my personality: coming to expect more of myself than I could sometimes give.

I was put to work every weekday morning either at my bedside or on the mats spread across each therapy room. On a daily basis the therapists performed range-of-motion stretches on my limbs and extremities. A comical aside: I originally thought it was called *Ranger* motion. In the narcissistic viewpoint of a nine year old, this seemed to confirm the fact that I rooted for the greatest hockey team in the entire universe! Anyway, with *range of* motion the muscles and joints are stretched to help avoid atrophy, the shrinking of muscles and stiffening of joints due to non-use.

Every accomplishment made in therapy was celebrated. When I put my shirt on that first time, a certificate was hung on the closet next to my bed commemorating the event. With great excitement, I was able to show off to my parents how I learned to roll over from a prone position, finally throwing enough of my upper body weight to one side that the momentum made my lower portion follow suit. They both expressed pride for my efforts. In these examples and countless others, I think the over-the-top praise and encouragement had less to do with the task itself than with the intention of making me strive for more.

By far my favorite form of therapy was recreation. The head of the recreation therapy department was a Chinese woman named Suzie Woo. Slim and highly Americanized, she had a dynamic personality to which you couldn't help but be drawn. A main highlight of each evening and weekend was the opportunity to play video games on the Coleco and Atari systems housed within her office. I could hold my own pretty well in such games as Jungle Hunt, Pitfall, and Pac-Man. This helped increase my popularity and soon I became friendly with a few other patients. We talked mostly about where we were from and shared our likes and dislikes around a variety of subjects. I remember sharing cassette tapes and being introduced to different types of music, including the never- before-heard genre of rap.

As the holiday season approached, the recreation department was instrumental in helping us provide gifts for our family members. There were jewelry-making workshops allowing us to create a necklace and earrings out of pearl colored beads. Not yet having refined my fine motor skills, I couldn't count how many times I stuck myself with the sewing needle which threaded the beads. It was all worth it in the end as the gifts went over as a big hit. To this day my mom still has the set.

That holiday season of 1984 was a trying time on a number of fronts. Gone were the Christmases where the gifts reflected a growing sports prowess. Just a year earlier I received a great deal of hockey equipment, including a street goal net, which I stumbled upon my parents constructing on Christmas Eve as I sleepily walked my way to the bathroom, from which vantage point I was provided a direct line of sight to the living room floor they were working upon. With my wits about me the following day, I put it all together. At eight years old I had definitive proof that my parents were indeed Mr. and Mrs. Kringle.

In addition to mourning such splendor of years past, dysfunction in family matters would rear its ugly head. Lest I get too far ahead of myself here, some background information is in order.

A single comfort of being holed up in the city was that my father's brother, George, was attending medical school at New York University. Being in such close proximity, it was not unusual for him to pay me much welcomed surprise visits. Such impromptu stopovers were something to look forward to.

Throughout the early part of my life I considered Uncle George to be way cool. The man could really fill a room and often commanded the center of attention. That being said, with the clarity of age these qualities would be redefined as him just being loud and obnoxious. At the time, though, our relationship held particularly tight due to the common bond of having a significant disability. His was an above-the-knee amputation of the right leg that occurred in 1982. Riding a motorcycle just outside his stationed naval base, my uncle struck a telephone pole.

The family trip we took to see him down in Maryland following his accident was not a pleasant one. My father never did get along well with his youngest sibling. I think it mostly comes down to a severe clash of personalities. George is all about spontaneity. His tendency is to react without thinking, acting very much on impulse in search of instant gratification. My dad is just the opposite, making calculated decisions with a conservative eye toward future consequences. In fact, an honest self assessment concludes that in this area I am definitely my father's son.

To his credit, my dad did not allow the hurtful feelings he had toward George or other members of the family unit in which he grew up to poison the relationships I would develop with them. That this had to be a somewhat difficult exercise in restraint I only later came to appreciate, as the dirty laundry of his upbringing was aired in bits and spurts throughout subsequent years.

Our miserable trip to Maryland culminated in a rather harrowing experience. On this cold and blustery day, our car crossed a highway overpass and came upon a patch of undetectable black ice. The vehicle (my grandmother's Chrysler New Yorker) became a bear to control and eventually found itself on two wheels, with me and my grandmother in the back seat being thrown violently to the right side. It was the type of moment when you don't realize what actually happened until it's over, even though consciousness was never broken. Through a bit of luck and Dad's expert maneuvering, all four wheels came to settle down again on the slick pavement. We were all shaken up to some degree but none the worse for wear physically. Ah, the precariousness of life. You gotta love it.

Throughout his many visits to RUSK, the fact of my uncle having a prosthetic lent an air of credibility to his words of support and encouragement. He became a role model that I believed worth emulating. In a sense, Uncle George had become my best friend. He was a friend who, unfortunately, would come to hurt me deeply.

As Thanksgiving approached, our house became more livable for me. In addition to a new hospital bed, my father had built a desk that covered some four feet of one wall and another two of the wrap-around corner, forming a precise right angle. Opposite the longer side and diagonal to my bed were a set of wooden sliding doors that revealed an inset walk-in closet.

At the halfway point of the bedroom ceiling one could faintly discern the line marking where a wall had previously separated my room from the den. The added space and more manageable sleeping quarters went a long way toward increasing my overall comfort level. Other amenities that helped included a complete expansion of the bathroom with the installment of a roll-in shower that I could access via a commode wheelchair.

Gatherings in the Hawkins home, by their very nature, were always small. As long as I can remember, my parents have always been home bodies not prone to traveling in social circles and establishing new friendships. Considering our small family, the holidays did not provide a significantly different atmosphere about our house. In this way a person's absence was highly conspicuous. Leading up to Thanksgiving, Uncle George promised to come and enjoy the festivities among company that would also include my grandparents from both sides of the family. It was billed as a happy event, as happy as it could be given my circumstance.

First I actually had to make it home. With my father working, my mom came to the hospital the evening before to pick me up. For assistance in transporting me, she brought with her Chipper's father, Charlie. Now it is pretty well established that Thanksgiving Eve is the busiest travel day of the year. Even without traffic, the hour-long drive from the city to home was in those days uncomfortable and somewhat difficult to bear. As it was, my balance was atrocious. Add to that a foreign seating environment, plus unpredictable vehicle motion, and you've got one unhappy camper.

Anything - such as traffic - that dragged out the trip only made matters worse. Distractions provided by someone not having to concentrate so much on the road came in handy, with games played to pass the time, including *I Spy* or *Twenty Questions*. Unfortunately, on that night nothing would help as the Long Island Expressway lived up to its nickname as the world's largest parking lot. Having little endurance for any particular activity, I was in both mental and physical agony as we pulled up the steep driveway of 1548 Carl Avenue some four hours after our journey began.

What made matters exponentially worse was that the following day my favorite uncle, the one in whose companionship I had put so much stock, failed to show up. I don't remember receiving so much as a regretful phone call that may have, at least in my eyes, exonerated such inconsiderate behavior. And while angered himself by the situation, I did not get the sense that my father was overly surprised.

Falling in the category of having really big balls or being just plain stupid, dear old Uncle George made his first contact with me more than a week after Thanksgiving. He came to the hospital at one of the worst possible times, popping in unexpectedly while I was having lunch with other patients in the large community room. As soon as I saw him seated directly across the table my emotions took over. Between heavy sobs I attempted to voice my disappointment about his neglect. In the midst of this tirade I threw my half eaten Italian Ice onto his lap. This display of theatrics caused quite a stir and drew the attention of supervising medical staff. With that, he got up and left. I saw I had one less person to count on, and our relationship from that point was never the same.

Enduring this incident I caught a glimpse that just because a person ought to act in certain ways does not necessarily mean they are going to. The same holds true when it comes to family. From such a standpoint there is added weight to what is said about the word "assume."

Now providing the offence in question isn't too egregious, as might be the case in terms of sexual or other abuse, I believe that in all relationships there exists an opportunity to wipe the slate clean and start over. After all, just like your friend's nose you can't really pick your family either. Fortunately, in my case overt abuse was never an issue. On the unfortunate side, before things could be formally patched up with Uncle George, contact was lost in his pursuit of a mainly nomadic lifestyle.

CHAPTER FIVE

Home

J ust when I thought I was out, they pulled me back in. Such was my sentiment when informed that one final test had to be performed before my formal discharge from RUSK could take place. I was pissed, to say the least. Here I thought I was in the clear, that my six months of intensive rehabilitation was finally coming to an end. Think again!

The last remaining procedure was an endoscopy. In a classic case of "me and my big mouth," my reported experience of persistent uncomfortable heartburn led to orders being written. Here was an affliction to which I had never before been subject. Originally the treatment of choice for the shooting pain through my esophagus was a Mylanta chaser provided each day in four hour intervals. Rather than send me home with this condition, the doctors thought it wise to decipher the nature of the problem so that a different treatment approach could be established. And though the timing was less than ideal, I *was* finding the particularly chalky taste of Mylanta increasingly difficult to bear. If only I'd known ahead of time what I was in for.

As it turned out, the procedure entailed having a garden hose-thick cable forced down my throat and into my stomach. To top off the experience, I had to be awake throughout as my swallowing action helped work the coil down with its attached camera. My insides were about to be broadcast via closed circuit television.

Prior to this invasion, my throat was swabbed with an anesthetic that had the most bitter of tastes. The intent may have been good but the experience of pain remained altogether too palpable. The results revealed my liver to be secreting excess bile. The treatment recommendation was the removal from my diet of caffeinated foods and drinks such as chocolate and soda.

Of particular note was that following my ordeal I was given a medication meant as a sleeping agent. I had a totally opposite reaction, becoming increasingly agitated and volatile to the point that I began cursing out my mother as she spoke with the presiding physician. Granted, the extent of my rant did not go beyond such language as "goddamn it," "damn," and "hell." Put together it sounded quite like, "Goddamn it Mom, why can't you just get me the hell out of this damn place!!!" That was an extremely bold statement coming from a child forbidden to use such language.

Once I finally came to several hours later, I could hardly talk from the soreness of my throat. As I began to make a valiant attempt at a sincere apology, Mom was quick to pick up on my intentions and implored me not to have any other concerns than to get some more rest. I'll always appreciate her understanding of the circumstances and not taking my outburst to heart.

Still, my experience of guilt could not be denied. All things considered, I had been a well-behaved child. Of course, that's not to say I didn't receive *any* punishments. In particular, there inevitably existed a power struggle whenever I was served a meal I did not like, or one that I didn't think I would like. A notoriously picky eater, I was stubbornly hesitant to try anything new. Armed with a precious few stand-bys, if given the choice my diet would have consisted entirely of grilled cheese, pizza, and Wheaties.

Especially disdainful to my taste buds were cooked carrots and hot dogs. A refusal to eat with these on the dinner menu would result in one of two outcomes. Behind door number one was being sent to my room, no doubt in very dramatic tears. These wouldn't flow for long though as it was not uncommon to find me moments later playing with my toys. Frustrated, and perhaps even a little amused by a lack of taking to heart the negative consequences of my behavior, the other mode of parental discipline was being made to sit at the dinner table until my plate was clean. My resilience, however, was continually underestimated. In fact, on multiple occasions I remember sitting there for hours, refusing to give in. The stonewall tactic would pay off as eventually it become time for bed. There would always be this light at the end of the tunnel. After all, what were Mom and Dad going to do, just leave me there?! An impasse reached, I was allowed to have something else to eat and go right to bed.

There were limits to my stubbornness, don't get me wrong. Think back, if you would, to times when you knew you were *really* in trouble. The signal for me was hearing my middle name. My mother sternly calling, "Derek Andrew Hawkins," was not something to mess with. One incident that provoked such ire involved being made to clean my room. It was messy, with toys strewn across the floor and on the bed, but I wanted to go outside and play. I raised suspicion by performing the quickest cleanup known to man. That's right; everything was thrown under the bed. You can be sure there was hell to pay for that one.

Yet throughout the entirety of my childhood I was never abused. I have no memory of being hit by family members or spoken to in a derogatory way. For this I am grateful, seeing the outcomes of such acts in my field of social work practice. I also don't recall harboring resentment prior to my injury. I realize this isn't always the case. To illustrate, one of my fellow playmates was fond of delivering the double "fuck you" hand signal to his mother behind her back. I would laugh along in a most uncomfortable way while unable to comprehend why he'd do such a thing.

Coming home for good as I did in the month of March 1985, my arrival coincided with the continuation of the academic calendar. Education had been a part of my weekday schedule of activities at RUSK. In fact, some of the very same materials I would have been working on back home in the third grade at Nokomis Elementary were provided by the school.

The first day at my hospital-based schooling produced a tirade of frustration as I was less than enthused with the quality of my handwriting. With one teacher assigned to teach the lot of us school-aged children, I felt pressure to succeed in the worst way. Albeit in a hospital setting, to attend school and participate in a *normal* activity provided an opportunity to prove myself. Competitive as I was, it meant the world to stand out and be good at something again.

Looking back, I want to shake that person and his unrealistic expectations. I want to scream, "RELAX, it is your first formal hour of classwork in some eight months and you will not, I repeat will not, be judged unfavorably by the quality of penmanship produced at this very instant." At the time I was calmed only with the reassurance that despite my disappointment I still wrote neater than any of my doctors.

Considering how much of an adjustment it was for me just to be home, I initially received home schooling from a teacher of my district. Based on my needs at the time, it became evident that a return to my "alma-mater" would not be plausible any time soon. In weighing the different options my parents were introduced to the idea of my attending an alternative school for the mobility impaired. Human Resources School (HRS) was founded by Henry Viscardi and is located, albeit now under a different name, in the town of Albertson on Long Island. A remarkable man, Mr. Viscardi devoted his life to assisting others like himself with physical disabilities. A major attraction of the school was the balance it maintained toward the sensitivities of people with disabilities while also honoring the human spirit present within each person, regardless of their physical capabilities.

HRS suited me well in almost every way, the sole exception being that the school was far from our house. Characteristic of Long Island traffic, there were times when the already lengthy forty-five minute one-way drive could take up to two hours to complete. With school hours being 10am to 4pm, that could make for a very long day.

Regarding the benefits, physical and occupational therapy services were available and provided much needed help toward increased strength and endurance. Then there was the return to a sense of normalcy with my academic role being restored to a school setting. Without the accompanying atmosphere, schoolwork does not quite feel the same when performed outside of the classroom. One needs to be among fellow students, each at their own desk being directed by a central figure, a teacher, who in the course of a lesson may utilize a dust laden chalkboard to help in its illustration.

Getting back to school also provided the opportunity to make some new friends. It was painfully obvious that the physical constraints of my injury left me little in common with my neighborhood peers. As with my old friend Chris DiMenna, after an initial spike in popularity from coming back home, those peers I had been closest to began to fade into the woodwork. While I was mad as hell at the time, I don't see how I can really blame them. Too much had changed. They knew it, as I eventually would.

Nothing brought this out more than an impromptu game of soccer in the neighborhood. I was invited, in my chair, to play goalie due to a shortage of players. To be given this chance was an honor I wanted to redeem with a good performance. Unfortunately, I was horrible. After the second quick score was let in I began to sob uncontrollably. My poor friends didn't know what to do with me. Since I had difficulty forming anything close to a coherent statement, they weren't quite sure what was wrong. I remember them being concerned that I had hurt myself. I was abruptly escorted home.

Far more than anything on my body, the part that hurt most was my psyche. In those moments of play, the physical differences that existed between me and the "normal" world became tangible. Gone were the fantasies that I could compete on their level. Born to me at that time was an underlying anger and jealousy toward the able-bodied, as well as depression over loss of the subtleties of movement I would never again experience. As a major blow to my self esteem, the degree of withdrawal from contact with my neighborhood cohort became mutual.

My first day of school at HRS was met with a great deal of anxiety. From the start I was an emotional wreck. Separation anxiety coursed through my veins with all the strength of straight black coffee fed intravenously. The mode of transport I'd be picked up in was the very undersized type of school bus that I had always heard made fun of when I was younger. At my old bus stop I joined in with those who rather derogatorily referred to these as "tart carts" for their propensity to bring the special education kids to class. Having to ride in one for the remainder of my compulsory education didn't exactly benefit an already dwindling sense of self worth.

On that day and for sometime thereafter, I was petrified of every bus driver whether they were black or white, male or female. Not that anything was done to validate my lack of trust. Most were extremely competent, safe drivers who conscientiously operated the lockdown equipment helping to keep my chair securely in place. Rather, I came to realize my fear stemmed from the lack of control I felt over potential situations. In those days I dealt a lot in potentials, primarily ones with substantially negative outcomes.

My mind was especially at its worst when I was alone or in the company of strangers. Scenarios ran through my head like a never ending loop of recorded tape. For instance, if one or both of my parents did not return to the car within a few minutes of making a purchase, I conjured an image of them having been murdered or kidnapped, with my helpless form left for dead. Another visual consisted of someone breaking into the car and taking me away to be killed or forever held from home. It was the latter scenario that rented significant space in my head with regard to what I imagined my bus drivers being capable of. Nothing of the sort ever did happen. Still, I was the worst sort of back seat driver, suspicion raised with every perceived missed turn or exit ramp.

Whatever fears I had about not being accepted at my new school were quickly put to rest. It was very hard **not** to make friends. For one, there was greater tolerance for physical disability as every student shared this characteristic in some shape or form. Many of us were in wheelchairs, with common conditions including Muscular Dystrophy and Spina Bifida. My disability was actually in the minority. There were also some students with mild diagnoses of Cerebral Palsy, or even birth defects, who were ambulatory with the aid of a handheld walker or crutches. Also conducive to a social atmosphere was the underwhelming size of the student body. The entire school, which in a single building taught grades K-12, maintained a total roster of approximately one hundred and twenty students. In the five years I spent there my class size never grew to more than eleven. Under such circumstances, one could not simply blend into the background. Trying to do so would produce the undesirable result of sticking out like a sore thumb.

Anxiousness aside, the start to my education at Human Resources School proved to be a highly positive experience. I was greeted warmly by my teachers and fellow classmates as I sought to finish out the school year with successful completion of the third grade curriculum. During the first day I became so distracted with my new environment, in fact, that the final bell came as a shock for which I was totally unprepared. With the rush of an incoming tidal wave, that increasingly familiar feeling of vulnerability returned as I had no idea how to reach the bus meant to take me back home. In a moment of sheer panic, I broke down and cried hysterically in front of everybody, students and faculty alike. Talk about a less than stellar impression to close out my first day!

All I could picture, though, was missing my ride and being left behind all night. I know, like that would ever be allowed to happen. Yet here's a glimpse into the bourgeoning mode of thinking I struggle against to this day. It is one of extreme cynicism, not waiting for, but *expecting* the other shoe to drop. Of course, in the above instance everything worked out and I arrived home just fine. Home: indeed, what a beautiful word.

CHAPTER SIX

That Time of Year

By no means am I one to put much stock in the field of astrology. I regard those whose passion consists of reading the stars with a great deal of skepticism. All in all it strikes me as wholly improbable that a person's behavior should be dictated by some nebulous outside force. This being said, there can be no doubt that I demonstrate certain characteristics unique to my designated birth sign. So much so, that posing the question to my wife of whether I am a true Gemini would result in such a vigorous nodding of her head you'd suspect it would fly right off her shoulders.

Illustrating the point that there are polar opposites in my personality, there's seemingly nothing else in the world with more power to instantly sour my mood than an accident involving my bodily functions. While I can largely tell when I have to go to the bathroom, once the feeling strikes I do not have the ability to hold it in for any significant amount of time. There's simply no two ways about it. When I have to go, *I really have to go.*

This feeling of having to relieve myself is not at all conventional, either. It can only be explained as a tingling sensation that emanates primarily through my head and shoulders. There's actually a medical term for it, called "dysreflexia." Being quite a mouthful it helps to sound out the word, and slowly. This term refers to quite an amazing defense mechanism of the human body. Usually when a person experiences pain or the need to relieve themselves, a signal is sent from that part of the body up through the spinal cord and to the brain. Here it registers that there is some sort of distress that requires varying degrees of attention. As in my case, when there is significant enough trauma to the spinal cord, this signal becomes blocked. Consequently, the brain is not made cognizant, in the conventional sense, of corrections needing to be made in areas of the body whose function is controlled below the level of injury.

Dysreflexia is the back-up generator of sorts that is relied upon at such times. Besides the notification of having to use the bathroom, there was an instance when the bare flesh of my leg came in contact with a hot pipe underneath the bathroom sink. With a scar to prove it, I've also spilled a scolding cup of hot water on my right inner thigh. Having no sensation, there is an obvious absence of direct pain. However, I become alarmed by other means such as involuntary muscle spasms and the same tingling sensation described above, only sharper in its presentation. The latter also occurs with the onset of a bladder infection, as do intense headaches, fever, and red blotchy skin when needing to urinate. Though not so much in my case, dysreflexia can also be accompanied by extreme elevations in blood pressure. I've witnessed this primarily when the level of injury was higher on the spinal column than my own.

As it relates specifically to going to the bathroom, by the time the tingling occurs there has already been a build up of pressure on my bladder or bowels that must be attended to rather quickly. It would be the equivalent of a more able-bodied person reaching the stage of having to cross their legs. In my case the level of injury renders my sphincter muscles beyond immediate control. With my accident I lost the ability to pucker up, so to speak.

A problem sometimes occurs in finding a suitable bathroom on time. In fact, the very first thing I must consider when going out anywhere is restroom availability. With learning to self catheterize, gone are the days of being able to wait and empty out a leg bag at a time that's more convenient. That previous arrangement had its own set of problems though, not the least of which was an increased feeling of being different with the knowledge of having a bag of piss attached to my leg.

Another variable that can complicate matters is the presence of a urinary tract infection (UTI). Though I commonly practice prior hand washing, I remain susceptible to infection due to consistent introduction of bacteria to the bladder. And while sterile self catheterization is ideal, for time and convenience sake it's in no way realistic. Until an antibiotic can be obtained and takes effect, with a UTI the window of opportunity between the feeling of having to pee and the actual event becomes even shorter. At least now, though, I get to participate in the more normalized process of peeing in the bathroom, instead of hoping that my urine makes it into a bag without any leaks or crimped tubing while I'm engaged in some other activity.

Now on those occasions when I'm not able to heed nature's call on time, I've been known to react rather violently to what in the grand scheme of things is not all that horrible. Having been through a lot with my injury, it has taken many years to reach a deep level of acceptance that I will never walk again. In exchange, all I ask is to not break a leg or develop a bad pressure sore. Another request is that I be allowed to make it to the freaking bathroom on time.

Understand that I do literally ask these things of myself. This may no doubt be difficult to comprehend. Truth is, it sounds a little unstable just writing it. I sometimes consider myself to have two bodies. The one I can control consists of the arms, hands, neck, head, and mind. Then there is the other, "lower body" that is mostly out of my control. While in the midst of a tirade I work myself up to believe, however irrationally, that the lower body has a mind of its own and is in many ways its own separate entity. I get angry at this part when it doesn't comply because I almost believe it acts on purpose.

Please, reader, don't stop here for fear I've gone mental. Far from crazy, the real phenomenon at work here is being confronted with the stark reality that I have a disability. And while impossible to deny, it is something I hate to consciously acknowledge. Realistically then, I don't see a time when I'll be totally calm and dismissive when something like a bladder (or god forbid a bowel) accident occurs, however rare it might be. Still, I have matured and no longer resort to statements of intent to hurt myself. Progress, not perfection, I suppose.

I don't want to lose the point of how absolutely true it is that throughout most of my waking days I do not carry with me the sense of having a disability. The wheelchair I get around in does not feel like a separate entity. It has developed into a part of me, serving as the legs that help me move from one place to another. Contributing factors include the comfort and ease of movement the chair provides. Constructed of lightweight titanium and weighing in at approximately fifteen pounds, I use the sports model wheelchair. Called a TiLite ZRA, it has a cushioned seat and back plus a compact design that provides a relatively short turning radius. Aesthetically, it is also pleasing, with an aerodynamic frame providing a certain "coolness factor." For my tastes, if someone is going to spend significant time in a wheelchair, then this is the brand to have, one that can be custom made to fit all body types.

In the beginning stages of using a chair I was at the mercy of utilizing one provided by the hospital. It was a behemoth of a thing made completely of solid metal save for the hard and unforgiving plastic seat and back rest. There was also a lack of maneuverability given the extreme weight and uncooperative wheel rotation. Having to sit in one of these you weren't afforded the luxury of *not* feeling like a disabled person.

Of course the most important reason for not feeling different from the able-bodied comes from the inside. In the same vein, it was a running debate among us kids at HRS on whether it was "better" to have been born with a disability or to incur one later in life, thereby having an opportunity to at least experience some time as an able-bodied person. The down side of a later disability is losing something that was once held dear. On the other hand and in support of being born with a disability, how can you miss something that was never had in the first place? Of course, it would seem the best option is never to have a disability, yet this obvious answer was lost to us at the time.

For me there is comfort in having once been able to walk. It helps my state of mind to describe my disability in terms of having incurred an injury. I prefer not to have the term "disabled" attached to my name at all, as to my ears it denotes someone inferior and helpless. These I am not.

To be injured is also more socially acceptable. No one likes to think in terms of having a disability, even though such a condition is bound to befall most people with the progression of time. On the other hand, everyone can relate to having been injured at some point. Granted, in terms of damage to the spinal cord, we're talking about one hell of an injury, unfortunately nothing a band-aid and peroxide can cure.

There's no doubt, though, that I feel most like a disabled person around the anniversary of my accident. Not even the worst diarrhea in the most awkward of social situations holds as much influence. During that time of year my mood is at its worst, and my reaction to every kind of stress is magnified to the thousandth degree.

While every June 28 is a chore to get through, there have been some milestones along the way that stand out as particularly difficult to stomach. For instance, there was a lot of crying after hitting year number one, no pun intended. With all the emotion of a raw nerve my parents and I huddled together, sobbing uncontrollably over what could no longer be denied: I was destined to spend the rest of my life in a wheelchair.

What made this more difficult to accept were dreams I had while at RUSK that weren't filled with much detail but the fact that in them I walked. Viewed with optimism at the time, they were considered a sign that never did come to fruition. Here the denial phase of loss was put to rest, with that first anniversary signifying the slaughter of any hope that my body would recover further on its own. Finality reluctantly set in and segued into an acute experience of anger, the second stage of grief and loss.

To borrow a Billy Joel song title, for many years I was "an angry young man." Content to linger just below the surface of my personality, this emotion began taking center stage on my anniversary date. The anger I felt was focused both inward and toward the driver who hit me. For the many years prior to getting the whole eyewitness story from Christopher, I blamed myself for my condition. I figured I must have done something to cause the accident. A bunch of "should" statements ran through my brain: I should have seen the car coming. I should have been able to get out of the way. I should have gone faster or perhaps slower. I should not have pressed so hard to be able to go in the first place. What's more, after viewing the driver's account of the accident I became haunted by dreams of rushing carelessly and without looking out into the street to meet my fate.

Less strong but present nonetheless was the blame I placed on the motor vehicle operator. There were unconfirmed rumors that he had been driving impaired. My mind ran with this. I hated him for the possibility of having been under the influence. He was an older man, just over the age of fifty. Here I hated him too for the slowing of reflexes and reaction time that accompanies advancement in age. I reckoned that if he were a younger man he'd have been able to avoid hitting me. Most of all I was angered by the fact that he had to be there at the exact spot and at the exact time which made it possible for the accident to occur in the first place.

The anger I experienced would show itself mainly in fits of rage and outbursts that included screaming and throwing things about my bedroom. Another behavior of choice was to topple over my wheelchair while sitting in bed. Of course this posed problems when I wanted to get up, but I was too angered to think so far ahead.

Coming down from this intense experience of feeling, I would be emotionally spent. What sometimes followed was a plea directed toward God himself that I would do just about anything to have my body restored to its optimal functioning. To my consternation, these prayers were never answered. This behavior of bargaining constitutes the third of five stages when it comes to grief and loss.

The fourth stage, depression, showed itself mostly at the approach of my tenth year with a spinal cord injury. This was a particularly trying time as it marked the point at which I spent more of my years on this earth as a person with a disability than otherwise. It was a smack of reality that hit with all the sting of a frigid, blustering wind. An entire decade spent in a wheelchair. Accepting this fact proved extremely difficult. Life had seemed to go by both fast and slow at the same time.

There I was having just completed my first full year of college, which followed the arduous and seemingly end-less task of getting through high school. And yet there was a little boy inside of me who had never left and needed to be mourned.

I was impossible to be around as my world was crumbling beneath the expectations I put upon it. Having come to the realization long before that it wasn't in the cards for my body to restore functioning on its own, I had nevertheless held out hope that technology would progress to the point of allowing me to one day walk again. To be sure, in those early years my picture of the future had me back on my feet again.

Adding fuel to this vision, I fed my mind with promises from spinal cord research that discovering the cure to paralysis was inevitable. The only major obstacle cited is what always seems to get in the way: money. Yet with each delivery of my subscribed spinal cord injury (SCI) newsletter there were interesting articles that docu-mented scientific theories requiring testing, along with subsequent years of trials on rodent specimens and, even-tually, humans. Unfortunately, the funding needed to sup-port such exhaustive work hasn't been provided by the government and has proven difficult to raise through pri-vate contributions.

Still, I did my best to remain optimistic. After all, it seemed reasonable enough to expect that something in the way of a cure would at least be developed in the ten years following my accident. Well, I'm now past year twenty-four and it seems I'm no closer to walking than I was back then.

When I become depressed I turn inward, desperately wanting to isolate myself from the outside world. This may be acceptable for a person who's truly alone in this world, someone with no family or friends. Otherwise, such behavior is bound to hurt others who least deserve it. The latter was by far the case with me.

That summer of 1994 found me at nineteen years old and in my first steady relationship with a woman. Heidi and I had met the previous summer at a day camp where we worked as recreation counselors. We are now married. It's a wonder she stuck around through the intense moodiness and desire to be alone that marked my behavior at that time. In my depressed state, it was not uncommon for me to dismiss her phone calls and avoid sustaining any significant contact with her or anyone else for that matter. Honestly speaking, I think I'd have been tempted to tell myself to take a hike.

At the very heart of my depression was not having made peace with the child that died on June 28, 1984. In order to move forward in my new life I needed to say goodbye to the old. And yet, like a tightened vice, my behaviors were making me stuck. A glaring example consisted of me rummaging through stacks of old photos, kept haphazardly unorganized, in search of ones that depicted myself as an able-bodied youth. In secret and behind the confines of my bedroom door I would gaze upon these pictures for hours on end, going so far as to construct my own photo album for easy reference. Here was a painful exercise that fed my depressive state, providing the energy it needed to flourish. Gazing upon my former self offered reminders of what I didn't have and could no longer do.

While difficult to admit, a part of me wanted to feel this way, had indeed gotten used to the overridingly negative mood festering inside of me since the turning of the '94 calendar year. After all, it seemed easier to wallow in the familiar than risk changing my thought and behavior patterns, despite the possibility of feeling better as a result.

Returning home for the summer after that first year of college, my attitude was not conducive toward functioning in close quarters with any human, least of all my parents, though they did their very best to be patient with me, as I had given them advance warning of how I was feeling towards this particular anniversary date. In fact, in an attempt to help, my mom expressed a sentiment that did not sit well with me.

That is, she thought I'd be wise to consider my anniversary as any other day, without such an emotional attachment. I felt she was utterly mistaken and she's since apologized for broaching the idea to begin with. After all, it would imply there was absolutely no reason to be overly happy about the approach of a birthday or some other special celebration such as Christmas or New Year's Eve. The last Thursday of November is not just *Thursday*, it's Thanksgiving, a day when you don't just do any old thing but instead gather with family and eat yourself to an advanced waist line. Unfortunately, my day has a conversely negative association that I can't wish away any more than I can deny feeling excitement and anticipation on Christmas Eve.

As patient as they were, everybody has their limits and my parents were no different. My emotional withdrawal and physical isolation reached a breaking point toward the conclusion of that summer, long past the time after my anniversary date when I usually returned to a sounder state of mental well-being. In the end it was my father who delivered the magic message that helped break me from this spell. He encouraged me to consider whether this was how I wanted to spend the rest of my life. If so, it was suggested I would die a lonely and very miserable human being. Although angered by his correctness, it was a message I'd take to heart.

Spurred by these words, escape from my incredible funk came via acknowledgement that throughout the course of this depression a nagging question burned inside of each waking day. Why me? What had I done to deserve this fate of being paralyzed for the rest of my life? I felt I must have done something wrong but I could not think of what it might have been. Finally it began to make sense that in my young life I wasn't capable of earning a punishment so severe based on my actions. I hadn't killed or maimed anybody. Nor can I recall having stolen or lied about anything of significance.

The road to acceptance, that most elusive and self-satisfying final stage of grief and loss, was paved by asking the question, "Why not me?" After all, what makes any of us so special that we think nothing bad should ever befall us? In fact, as a species it occurs to me that we humans tend to think a little too highly of ourselves. From what I've seen there often exists an attitude of 'that's not going to happen to me.' That line of thinking works until, dare I say, it does happen to you. We don't like to consider our vulnerabilities. Nor can I say that I'm much different. Even now and with everything I've been through there is an occasional inclination to not wear a seatbelt while a passenger on local errands. Of all people who should know better, right?

Another favorite complaint of mine used to be that what had happened to me wasn't fair. Surely there must be some order and justice to the world that should have given me some protection from the cruelties reserved for the "bad" people in life. That this was not the case caused me to question my belief in God. I was convinced that if there was a God he would have been watching over me and in doing so would've prevented in some way the accident from becoming a reality. If God was as powerful as advertised, he would have intervened on my behalf. Riding my bicycle as a child, I'd look up to the sky in full motion and try to spot heaven through an array of clouds on an otherwise sunny day. Now in my altered state, I thought I understood why it could never be seen.

From the perspective of acceptance, I came to have an entirely different understanding of my situation. In my reframing of life events I have removed from my vocabulary altogether the descriptors of "should" and "fair." In regards to my accident, I have come to grips with it being an unfortunate event that could have happened to anybody. I have moved away from the contention that life is meant to be fair.

Life just is. I introduced peace to my life for the first time when I embraced this concept. The process of healing had roots from which to grow. No longer did I place such considerable blame on myself or others. The new philosophy that served me well ran along these lines: shit happens and I needed to make the best out of an unfortunate, but not life ending, situation. In my own soul-searching analyses of my father's message, I came to a deep understanding that this life I have been given is limited. I could not go back and change what had already occurred. The best I could do was to proceed with what I had.

Now for the sake of argument, let's say I got my wish and the accident never occurred. Sounds great, right? Who is to say, though, that some other tragic event wouldn't have happened a month from then that would have resulted in the loss of my life? In this way I'm grateful to have been recovering in the hospital at a time I otherwise would have been dead. From this perspective getting into that accident could have actually *saved* my life instead of ruining it. Given the opportunity I'd choose paralysis over nothingness any day of the week.

By far and without question, the single biggest obstacle that had traditionally gotten in the way of embracing acceptance as a real possibility was equating it with liking the circumstance I found myself in. I have since learned to think differently. Accepting something really has nothing to do with liking it. Instead it is the ability to acknowledge that you *don't* like a particular outcome, with a conscious decision to not let the undesirable result become a personal albatross. In my own case no one will ever hear me say that I like not being able to walk. My condition is not something to which anyone in their right mind would aspire. However, it also is not a death sentence. There is still plenty that I can do. Today I choose to focus more on these abilities than my limitations. In order to have moments of true happiness, there's really no other choice.

Sound a little too good to be true? Well indeed it is. Having worked my way through the five stages of grief and loss in no way makes me the poster boy for perfect mental health. After all, reaching the final stage of acceptance doesn't come close to assuring that anger and depression will never again rear their ugly heads.

Regarding this chapter title of the same name, over the years I've discovered that the extent these moments linger is in direct proportion to how I choose to spend my no good, horrible, very bad day. The most important lesson learned has been to minimize the stress I am under to the greatest degree possible. For this reason, I no longer go to work on my anniversary.

As a social worker I have a very stressful, mentally draining occupation. And, like most jobs, in order to be effective I must be wholly present. This was especially the case having worked my way up from a line clinician to a supervisor, and then even further to program coordinator. At work, my time was demanded throughout the entire duration of my shift, whether by my boss, the staff I supervised, or most importantly, my clients.

Even now, in my not-as-taxing position of case manager, with the accident on my mind I am not an effective worker. Responsible for a multitude of job tasks, the last thing I can afford is to engage in a favorite anniversary day pastime, daydreaming. At the mere glimpse of a clock, my mind tends to wander toward thoughts of what I'd be doing at that exact moment back on June 28, 1984. Time becomes lost that should be devoted to work-related activities.

There's plenty of work to go around, too. Having held full-time stints at three organizations, I've come to appreciate that even if it's not entirely universal, most healthcare positions are dominated by an exorbitant amount of paperwork with set due dates. Due to the nature of the business, if a person is not already behind they are most surely right on the brink. And while failure to meet certain deadlines is sometimes explainable, personal lateness of any kind does not sit well with me. Those times I even get a sense of it result in significantly elevated stress. Having risked this being part of past anniversaries did nothing but add to the depression and anger experienced on those "special" days.

Also tied into my self-directed isolation from work is the weight and magnitude of what that day represents, the experience of a death without actually dying. That's correct; as much as anything, June 28 has become a day of mourning. To be sure, I've been known in some years to visit the approximate spot where the accident occurred, the exact location no longer accessible due to expansion of the town's railroad station upon that area. Anyway, there I'd park, usually remaining in my car to contemplate what was and what could have been. To say I'm overcome with emotion more than twenty years after the fact would be grossly inaccurate. However, that's not to say I am completely emotionless. What I feel most now is sorrow for the little boy who died that day and the pain he must have felt.

Considering the overwhelmingly dramatic turn my life took on that eighteenth day past my ninth birthday, I cannot help but feel there were two entirely different people, in both body and mind, from before to subsequent the impact with the vehicle. That person from before is dead to me. I acknowledge his existence only on the anniversary of his death as a way of paying my respects and nothing more.

Finally, this ties into a last, but certainly not least, reason for taking advantage of a paid day off. That is, coping with this weighty issue leaves me with zero tolerance for bullshit. To varying degrees throughout my career I have dealt with people's bullshit, whether from staff or clients. Regarding the latter, it especially applies to my work with addicts, as the drug and alcohol population is in general (of course there is room for exception) a highly manipulative and dishonest group. The patience and understanding I have in reserve on most any other calendar workday becomes nonexistent. Regarding people I have worked with, from my experience some emotionally unhealthy people gravitate toward the field of social work. While their hearts may be in the right place with a codependence toward helping others, they fail to realize that without taking care of one's own issues, there will be a significantly decreased opportunity to effect positive change in others.

Nowadays my typical anniversary is spent at home. If it falls during the week, I schedule in advance either a personal, sick, or vacation day. This is actually preferable to it falling on a weekend, when at least half of that coveted time off would be devoted to melancholy. For, like the tightest cocoon, while perhaps not *physically* alone, I become very much wrapped within myself.

Anticipating this expected moodiness has led me to abide by certain steadfast rules. First, I try to sleep late. The fewer hours I have to deal with, the better. Second, I don't go out anywhere. One year, in my not so infinite wisdom, I took a ride on my hand propelled bicycle to prove that I couldn't be deterred from living the same as any other day. There was a price to pay, as I was overcome by a strong sense of eeriness that rendered the bike ride thoroughly unfulfilling. Finally, the last of my rules is that I don't answer the phone or the door unless absolutely necessary. "Like a hole in the head" is how I need to explain away my less than outgoing personality. Though besides my wife's presence there is one other exception, the expected and welcome call from my mother.

Since I moved out of my parent's home at the age of twenty-five, my mom has made it a point to check up on me with words of support and encouragement. She chooses to acknowledge that this is a very bad day for me, and I love her for it. Otherwise, I'd tend to feel even more alone than I would like, as there are few others beside my parents who share the history of all I've been through. Over the phone my mom is able to listen and commiserate as to the heaviness filling the air like on no other day. There is no crying, only acknowledgement of what the day represents and the need to persevere until tomorrow, when like the purest helium, the air will seem considerably lighter and a whole lot easier to breathe.

Interestingly enough, though they reside under the same roof, I never get a similar call from my father. As to exactly why I don't hear from him, I have no idea. It's not something that has been talked about, nor can I say I'm hurt by it either. Ultimately, my best guess is that he just doesn't want to go there. As lead evidence all I have to go by is that in the past, when in earshot of such conversations between me and my mom, he chose not to join in or even ask what we were talking about, as he usually would otherwise. But who am I to judge? And while I know he must go through a lot too, from an outside glance you'd never tell.

With that said, an altogether desirable circumstance that has come with the passing of time is the lessening duration that I find myself impacted by the anniversary of my accident. It has gotten so that I can effectively turn the page and return to normal functioning once the clock turns to 12:01 a.m. on June 29. This was far from the case in the earliest years when I would literally experience a season of sorrow extending from the end of May through the 4th of July. That my depressed state has been localized to a single day or so is a blessing. At least now I can enjoy my birthday to the fullest.

Truth be told, I don't want *not* to be affected in any way on my anniversary. For one thing, I need to be reminded that I once did walk, as it helps to lessen the intimidation that might otherwise be experienced when interacting with the able-bodied. With constant reminders imposed on those with disabilities as being different, considering myself an equal to the able-bodied is no easy task. Finally, it also helps to remain in tune with just how much I've been able to overcome. While I would be hard pressed to refuse an opportunity to return to the age of 7 or 8, you couldn't pay me enough to go back to being a month past nine years old.

CHAPTER SEVEN

First Love

In its social aspects Human Resources School was like any other. There were cliques, to be sure, though they numbered a select few. What else could be expected of a school that had in its entire enrollment just over one hundred students? The main determinant of who was considered cool had its origins in the layout of the building.

Human Resources School had two floors. The first floor held grades Kindergarten through Sixth Grade. On the second were the Junior High and High School students. Perceived as royalty, the ultimate status symbol was to be one of those upstairs. Students there sat taller in their chairs, and for the most part were more impressive in their maneuverability due to strength that comes with age.

No matter what the intentions, a rift was sure to occur between those sixth graders moving up and the younger friends they were forced to leave behind. After all, it was considered almost social suicide to sustain friendships with the downstairs students, as if they were a different breed of people altogether. To be fair also, being cut off from the K-6 classrooms made the maintaining of previous friendships more difficult in the first place. It was under these circumstances that I met a boy named Jay, my first best friend since the accident.

Having started in the latter stages of the school year at HRS, my arrival coincided with the last remaining months of Jay's bond with his best friend at the time, who would be progressing to the 7th grade. Being in the same class, Jay and I became close rather quickly. He had a bone disease that rendered his limbs extremely thin. The condition also limited his size, so that at full height he would only grow to be some four feet tall. Unable to support his fragile limbs, Jay used a wheelchair for mobility.

The coolest thing about Jay was how fast he was. At full speed he propelled his chair to a virtual blur. He was also very outgoing, with an infectious laugh towards which you couldn't help but gravitate. There was also a mean streak to Jay, a dark side to his personality that made you glad to be his friend rather than his enemy. He possessed the most amazing charisma that could make you feel intimidated in his presence when he wanted you to feel that way. Do you know people like this? At first appearance, with his emaciated limbs and short stature, you'd think he would be a push-over in a fight. It was the wild look in his eyes, though, that made you reconsider, a glare that begged you never to witness his bad side.

In my heart I believe that losing his best friend was a bitter experience in Jay's young life, from which he was slow to recover. Whether conscious of it or not, he seemed to have made a personal vow to do his best and avoid being hurt that way again. For instance, from my initial full school year onward, Jay assumed the role of the followed rather than the follower. Furthermore, the friends he chose from that point had less than dominating personalities, in which I led the way. With self esteem akin to being on the ground floor of a skyscraper high-rise, I considered it a personal victory for any peer to take the initiative and simply say hello to me. So when Jay actually recruited me to be part of his inner circle, I felt only happiness and a true sense of belonging.

Throughout the 4th and 5th grades the darker aspects of Jay's personality became more prevalent. Wanting to remain his friend, I chose to ignore the warning signs, of which there were many. For one thing, he had a penchant for stealing. And although I knew better, with my desire to be liked I soon found myself joining in the practice of taking as our own the pens and other school supplies of fellow students. Sometimes we even risked swiping items from teachers' desks. This went on for quite a while, until someone finally told on us. Jay remained stoic throughout our teacher's interrogation right in front of the class. Under the pressure I cracked like an easy safe, breaking down in a fit of sobs.

Ultimately, it seemed I was not cut out for the life of a criminal. Yet to my surprise, the sign of weakness I displayed did not strain our friendship. If anything, it was a doorway through which Jay learned just how easily I might be influenced by intimidation. Such meekness attracted him greatly. What ultimately *did* cause irreparable damage to our relationship is a tale as old as time itself.

Her name was Maria, and she was the most beautiful girl upon which my eleven year old eyes had ever gazed. In what could only be described as one of the cruelest of life's circumstances, Maria was born with the condition of Muscular Dystrophy (MD), a genetic disorder that severely damages muscle cells and tissue. It does so in a progressive manner that often renders an individual defenseless against an early demise. Of the most common types of Muscular Dystrophy to affect young people is Duchenne's. Those unfortunate enough to inherit this particular disease generally do not live to see their 25th birthday.

Maria was just about the sweetest, most unassuming person you'd ever hope to meet. She was pretty too. Man, was she ever pretty. She was petite, had long, wavy brown hair, and smooth unblemished skin of olive complexion. You could lose yourself in her wide, green eyes. Maria was a year older than I and highly sought after by the other boys at school. It was easy to consider myself fortunate that it was me she found interesting. She was to be my very first girlfriend.

Of all the positive aspects of Human Resources School, the one ranked highest among us kids was the bi-monthly after-school program held on Friday nights. It was aptly named "Friday Night Recreation." "Friday Night Rec," as we called it, afforded the students an opportunity to socialize outside of the school setting. This was important given the extremely wide catchment area served by the school. Transporting students from points some forty miles away, it was a whole different world from a public school education, where a child's friends might all live within a few blocks of their own home. To lend some perspective, in the two years we were together Maria and I had only been to each other's houses once. Her parents' house in Seaford was a solid forty-five minute drive from where we lived in Holbrook.

During the Friday night program at HRS there weren't any real school activities that took place. In fact, the main attraction of the evening was the playing of wheelchair hockey. This was an organized event consisting of six teams that competed for the end-of-the-year right to be declared school champions. It was a much sought after symbol of prestige. I played every year and remember being on the tournament winning team at least once. I was always pegged for a defenseman, a position I would grow to like even though I coveted being goalkeeper. That role was usually reserved for the senior classmen. The teachers who stayed late to watch over the participating students became our coaches. It was interesting, the interactions we could then have in such a different atmosphere.

Those students who did not play hockey (or whose team wasn't playing at that time) could take advantage of playing games in the computer lab or simply hanging out and talking in the cafeteria. This is where I could often be found with Maria. We were joined at the hip, the two of us. I loved to spend time with her, making her laugh with the stupid jokes I would tell. She was naturally shy and very timid, the perfect match for my own personality.

It was during one of those hanging out episodes that we contemplated the idea of having our first kiss. It would be the first for both of us, and it ended up being the most awkward of moments. For a location we ventured off into a little alcove at the far end of the cafeteria, sufficiently beyond anyone's direct line of sight. We then positioned our chairs side by side and as close together as possible. By the tender age of thirteen Maria had lost the strength needed to push herself around with any real authority, so she operated a motorized wheelchair that sat lower to the ground than my own manual chair. So there we were, with me looking down upon her. We made idle chit chat for what seemed like eons. It finally came to the moment of truth, the bewitching moment when if it was going to happen, it had to go down soon. And so after one more round of questions on whether we were both okay to proceed, I leaned myself over to the left. She stayed mostly still, shyly turning her head up in my direction. We both closed our eyes and I moved in closer, aiming to secure the defining moment of my social life. A current of adrenaline coursing through my veins, my mind became a jumble of confusion as my mouth made direct contact *not* with her mouth. You see, I had kissed Maria's nose. Luckily I was able to collect myself, correct my position and give her a peck on the lips.

What followed was not a plethora of stolen kisses between classes, or make-out sessions in favorite hideaway places. Maria and I jointly agreed to have rushed into the whole thing in the first place. Despite her assurances to the contrary, I could tell she was uncomfortable and only went through with it to please me. I, in turn, regretted having pressured her in any way toward doing something for which she wasn't entirely ready.

Instead of this coming between us, we became closer than ever. She would give me studio portraits of herself and write "I Love You" on the backs of them. I saved them and now they occupy a special place in my memory box. She would also write "I Love Derek" on the bottom of all her shoes. I simply can not overstate how good a person she was. Maria was without an agenda when it came to her interest in me. Such knowledge began to inspire in me the confidence that I had something positive to offer another human being. Added together, these facts made even more regrettable the circumstances surrounding our breakup.

It all started with a rumor. I'd venture to say that in any small social setting with less than fully mature people, there is a tendency for everyone to be in each other's business. The students at HRS were no different, myself included. Against the backdrop of this reality, word got back to me in sixth grade that Jay, my supposed best pal, was putting the moves on my girl.

This was all too much for me to handle. Handle it I did though, albeit in the worst possible way. Rather than being addressed in a rational manner by approaching Jay or Maria with a level head, I instead let my insecurities run wild as a rabid dog. Afraid all along of her being taken away from me, it was as if I couldn't believe the rumor *wasn't* true. I made up my mind that something had to be going on between them, even though I had no supportive evidence whatsoever.

My relationships with Jay and Maria deteriorated significantly. Jay did not take kindly to my open accusations. That anyone would ever challenge him automatically placed that person outside his social circle. Furthermore, in Jay's view of the world, you were either with him or against him. There was no middle ground. Therefore, I quickly found myself taking the role of his mortal enemy. In hindsight, perhaps it was my fault for remaining friends with anyone I would think capable of stealing my girlfriend in the first place.

When it came to Maria, I began to isolate myself from her with increasing regularity. I could tell she was hurt and confused by my actions. After all, she really had done nothing wrong! My behavior would sink to even lower depths as I attempted to pin the demise of our relationship on her shoulders. In what would be our last extended conversation, I "guilt tripped" Maria into believing that I was breaking up with her because she did not pass the test of coming to spend time with me. It was true that with her extreme shyness it was I who initiated most of the contact between us. Even so, this was one of the most bullshit excuses of all time. The truth is that I wouldn't want to spend time with *myself* given how standoffish, how emotionally and physically unavailable I had been toward her for quite some time. Acting like a total bastard, I put all the blame on her. In a final act of indignity, instead of doing so in person, I communicated all of this to Maria over the telephone.

By this time I had also taken advantage of my new-found self confidence and formed friendships with a group separate from the followers of Jay. They all seemed to have the same thing in common: for whatever reason they also found themselves outside Jay's good graces. It just may be that simple, that some people hate others for no good reason. Whatever the case, becoming more invested in these relationships seemingly put to rest any hope for reconciliation.

Soon our two groups waged a sort of war against each other, Jay and I designated as the respective leaders. Jay was relentless in taking every opportunity to bang his chair against mine. As if that weren't enough, his buddies (and my former friends) got into the act as well. Let me tell you, it's no fun getting run into by a motorized wheel-chair weighing a few hundred pounds. While it was harder to get away with during class, particular liberties were taken during physical education. It was for this reason that, while playing sports such as hockey or adaptive soccer (played with a bigger ball pushed around by hand), I took the position of goalie. Of course, it helped that I could hold my own doing so. Football was a different situation that left me highly vulnerable. In fact, it wasn't unusual to take hits from my own teammates!

Subjected to this constant harassment, I began to feel smaller in stature than my height-challenged arch nemesis. Whatever confidence I had built up seemingly vanished when in Jay's presence. He ultimately wanted to fight me and wasn't shy about making this known to anyone who'd listen.

One thing already proven about me is that I was no fighter. Always the more passive type, physical aggression did not appeal to me. Unfortunately, this trait followed me and was interpreted as a form of weakness. Again, from my earliest memories, I was taken advantage of as a result, picked on at times almost without mercy.

Though even to my own surprise, I did have limits. As a seven year old I found myself confronted by a neighborhood bully, whose incessant name calling was making me look the fool in front of my peers. Not seeing any other option, I marched up on the property of my heckler to try and make him stop bothering me. Just how I planned to accomplish this was beyond my immediate comprehension. As things turned out, before I knew it my head was repeatedly introduced to his concrete front stoop. A swift decision, as ever; I was led home by the onlookers, face bloodied and ego damaged.

Given these less than spectacular results, my parents saw fit to have me learn self defense. With this in mind I began to take lessons in karate. Overall, the experience was a positive one that paid almost immediate dividends. In these classes I received the proper teachings that violence is to be used only as a last resort in defending oneself from physical attack. Now if only more people would abide by this rule...

Anyway, the onset of my accident curbed my ability to learn more advanced techniques beyond the most basic of punching styles. Thankfully it proved to be all I'd need, as boarding the school bus one day at the age of eight found me sitting in the seat directly ahead of a bus stop antagonist, relentless with his teasing and juvenile disparaging comments. These I did my best to ignore, words not being able to hurt me and all. Soon thereafter I became subject to the most annoying tapping on the back of my head. By this time I was getting real worked up until finally it became too much to take.

Before the bus even had a chance to resume its school-bound journey I turned around and with one motion tucked an upturned fist in close to my side. Demonstrating impeccable technique, I gave him a karate punch to the mouth by twisting my hand while thrusting the arm forward for the most solid and swift of connections. He never saw it coming. From the moment I saw the blood on his lip I thought for sure I was going to be in big trouble. Like a good little bully who is finally put in his place, the recipient of my blow went up crying to the bus driver. I never liked to be in trouble so I looked on with trepidation for what might be the consequence awaiting me. To my relief, the driver verbalized that she had heard his taunting and pretty much felt he deserved what he had gotten.

Much like the above example, the stress of being constantly accosted by Jay was starting to get the better of me. It was beginning to show in my attitude at home.

My parents knew that Jay and I were no longer friends but I did my best to downplay the extent to which our relationship had deteriorated. The last thing I needed was my parents getting involved with the school and me gaining the reputation of a tattle-tale. Besides, I really didn't think it would do any good. Jay's name calling and chair crashing, witnessed by teachers, was met with rather bland threats and unheeded warnings for him not to do it again. So on and on the abuse continued. The only resolution appeared to be accepting Jay's challenge to a fight. I could sense from my new group of friends that there was a question being raised whether I had enough guts to actually go through with it. Against my better judgment, I finally relented.

The showdown that ensued was by no means one for the ages. First of all, the fight took place before the start of the school day in a seldom-used bathroom on the downstairs level. Jay and I each had a friend present to serve as witnesses. Second, I never threw a significant punch, mostly holding my arms up in a defensive posture. This only served to infuriate my opponent. Jabs to my stomach were deflected by a brace I wore at the time meant to help correct the curvature of my spine, scoliosis, which developed as a result of my injury. After a few shots landed to my shoulder and head, Jay asked if I wanted mercy. At that point I was glad to concede a fight I wanted no part of to begin with. To my rather pleasant surprise, I was not ostracized by my friends as a result of this loss. Just standing up to Jay had been a victory in their eyes.

It's truly a shame any of this nonsense even had to take place. If ever there was a student body deserving of being more closely knit, it should have been that at Human Resources. Enrollment made one vulnerable to confronting the issue of personal mortality. There were too many student losses in the few years I spent there and later heard about after my departure. It wasn't only the deaths with which we contended, though these were bad enough. Given the degenerative conditions of some students, it was also difficult to witness the progressive loss of ability from one school year to the next. Friends would return from summer vacation unable to walk on their own or reaching the point of having to use a motorized wheelchair. The ability to independently feed one's self might also be lost. Instead of growing stronger with age, it was in these cases that the body would become weaker and considerably frailer.

I can recall a particularly poignant conversation with a fellow student with whom I had a neutral relationship. His name was Andrew Desoto and he was always very sickly looking. Unable to move his arms and legs, Andrew had, since I'd known him, been able to operate his motorized chair only by a joystick secured just under his chin. Becoming unable to perform even this simple task, Andrew confided to me out of the blue that he wished he could be me. I couldn't believe he would say such a thing and actually mean it. After all, at the time I wanted to be just about anyone else *but* me. With this in mind, I quickly dismissed the idea that this was something he could seriously have wanted. Sadly, in a matter of a few weeks Andrew passed away.

Over two decades later I believe I understand where Andrew was coming from. How hard it must have been for him to realize that the end was near. It must be a difficult thing, to remain stoic approaching death, considering the lack of opportunity to lead a rich and full life. It makes me wonder now whether I'm taking full advantage of the opportunity not afforded to everybody in this world. Considering how others such as Andrew would kill to be in my or your position, isn't there an obligation not to let this time on earth go to waste? The answer to me is a resounding yes.

Regarding my first love, it was in my junior year of high school that I learned of Maria's failing health. For many people with Muscular Dystrophy, the complications associated with this diagnosis end up killing them. Already in a weakened state, the body has a harder time recovering from sickness. In Maria's case, it is my understanding she had a difficult time shaking a severe cold, so much so that it eventually progressed to pneumonia. This landed her in the hospital for quite some time. News of her illness hit me particularly hard considering how things were left between us; me leaving HRS without extending her a formal apology for my despicable behavior. In desperation I sought a way to make things right before it became too late.

The most ideal situation would've been to have a conversation with her in person. Unfortunately, she had a trachea inserted as a breathing aid, and as such it was difficult for her to communicate. It also got back to me through her best friend at HRS, with whom I had remained in contact, that Maria did not want to be seen in her current state. For this I couldn't blame her. Under these circumstances, I pursued the only other option available to me. I wrote her a heartfelt letter.

Writing that letter was a very cathartic experience. I took the opportunity to detail how I'd been completely at fault for our breakup, how I missed her so much and hoped more than anything for her recovery. It was with tremendous satisfaction that I learned Maria's mother had read the letter to her in the hospital, and that the message it conveyed was warmly received. It truly meant the world to me that Maria did not die with any guilt or malice towards me. In fact, she was able to leave the hospital and return to school, albeit with a respirator attached to her wheelchair due to continued difficulty breathing on her own. Shortly after, though, Maria's parents decided to move the family back to their native Italy. I was crushed by this news, having held out some hope that we had time to reestablish a friendship. Unfortunately it wasn't meant to be. The news of her move was the last I ever heard of Maria.

Given her condition and its associated life expectancy, I know she must have passed some time ago. Even so, it remains a difficult thing with which to come to terms. I am truly saddened by the prospect of Maria not being part of this world. I think of her often as having the best personality I've ever known besides my wife's. I guess it's true, that you never do forget your first love.

CHAPTER EIGHT

On Death's Doorstep

Aside from the accident itself, I've had the misfortune of enduring additional near death experiences. As if the first wasn't enough! While difficult to go through at the time, I must admit to learning a lot from each of them. As the old saying goes, what doesn't kill you only makes you stronger.

One of these instances occurred in January 1986. From a sports standpoint that was a banner year, with two of my favorite franchises winning championships. The "Amazin' Mets" pulled out a miraculous World Series comeback for the ages, made legend by a routine grounder scooting through the legs of Bill Buckner. Then there was the New York Giants football team claiming Super Bowl XXI, quarterback Phil Simms putting on a clinic in passing accuracy as the team charged their way past John Elway and the Denver Broncos.

Yet on this cold and dreary winter's day in January, the theme of sports was the farthest thing from most people's minds. The nation, including me from a hospital bed, witnessed the explosion of the *Challenger* space shuttle on live television. Like my parents generation with the J.F.K assassination, prior to the attacks of 9/11 it was the *Challenger* tragedy of January 28, 1986 that stands out as one of those dates you never forget. I wonder if, like me, an overwhelming majority of my cohort remember where they were and what they were doing at that exact moment. Sadly enough, due to both mechanical and human error, the vaunted shuttle never made it beyond Earth's atmosphere. In what can only be described as surreal, no sooner did the launch commence than before a nation's eyes the fuselage caught fire and disintegrated down toward its ocean grave. Dead on impact, years later it was eerie to learn that conditions within their compact capsule supported the astronauts' continued consciousness throughout the explosion. More than likely they were aware of their rapidly approaching fate.

Back to me, out of the hospital for almost two years, I required corrective back surgery for my scoliosis. As already mentioned, my particular type of structural scoliosis was caused by my injury. Other known causes of this irreversible type include the conditions of spina bifida and cerebral palsy. Nonstructural, reversible scoliosis also exists and is attributed to muscle pain or spasm, appendicitis, and differences in leg length.

Though the personally-fitted brace strapped around my chest and torso helped keep my spine in alignment, such a thing was not without significant disadvantages. First, the very nature of being strapped in somewhat tightly was enough to restrict my breathing. Also, the plastic edges (or sometimes metal, as I tried many different brace designs) were bound to dig into the skin and leave their marks, especially around the armpit and hip areas. Each of these factors caused me to remain in an almost perpetual state of discomfort. Then there was the extra time it took being helped into the brace and the degree to which it restricted my movements. All in all, I pretty much hated every moment of functioning this way on a daily basis. And to think I was due to wear such a brace long into my teenage years, until my body stopped growing. Surely there had to be a better way. Fortunately there was, whose rewards I'd reap in the long run. Having almost killed me, the short term results were not nearly as positive.

Referred to a back specialist, I was evaluated by a neurologist in New York City who was a leader in the field of spinal fusions, a particularly invasive surgical procedure in which two metal rods are imbedded on either side of the spinal column and held in place by a wire wrapping. The anticipated outcome would be a permanently straightened back no longer requiring the aid of a brace or other such contraption. Of all the operations I had undergone, this ranked as one of the biggest. At stake was the potential for significant quality of life improvement, though whenever dealing with something as significant as the core of the central nervous system there is also some risk involved. With such a sensitive mechanism, the slightest mishap could result in increased loss of function or even death.

As the scheduled date of my surgery approached I became increasingly nervous. Of course, it didn't help that the older kids on my HRS bus route would relate some of the horror stories they "knew" of other people who had the same operation. These ran the gamut from infection to mortality. Though I believe them now to have had some fun at my expense, at the time, the tales they spun were unnerving enough that I eventually broke down in heavy sobs to my mom just days prior to the main event.

The surgery was performed at The Hospital for Special Surgery in Manhattan and the procedure itself was a success. In fact, when I saw my parents for the first time in the recovery room, it was with great satisfaction that they answered "yes" to whether my back looked straight. Having been pulled apart and put back together again from neck to tailbone, I was held overnight in the recovery room with an attendant by my bedside upon whom I could call in case of emergency. Sleep was hard to come by in my compromised state. While I was provided with a fair amount of medication for pain relief, I remember still feeling fairly uncomfortable. Not helping matters were the screams that could be heard from an even younger patient, whose bed was stationed not far from my own.

I must have dozed off at some point, only to wake in a state of absolute panic. For the life of me, I could not catch my breath. Try as I might, I could not get any air to pass through some severe congestion in my lungs. It felt like I was drowning, sans submersion in a surrounding body of water. Choking on my own mucus and unable to talk, I soon began to flail my arms. Finally drawing the attention of my bedside aide, I allowed myself a brief moment of hope that everything was going to be all right. Like the last failing ember of a great fire, that glimmer was rather short lived. It turned out my salvation lay in someone who spoke not a word of English.

The thought intruded into my panic-stricken brain that I just might be a goner. The more I tried to get my point across to my solely Spanish speaking aide, the more frazzled *she* became. All the while, I still could not clear my airway. It didn't feel like long before I'd pass out. On the heels of this reality, help was finally called for and a whole team of doctors and nurses were soon rushing to my side.

To be clear, I am not a masochist. I neither enjoy nor welcome the infliction of pain to my body in the least respect. That said, to restore the ability to breath I was willing to endure the most severe of tortures. What my lips couldn't speak my eyes screamed, *"Cut me, bleed me, and stick a needle in my eye if it should lead toward the sweet drawing of air!!!"* As it actually happened, a tube was forced down my throat for the suctioning of collected phlegm from my lungs. What an absolutely welcome relief.

Normally, at that age I had to be coached through any such procedure. Yet in my desperate state, the thought of needing such assistance never crossed my mind. This brings me to conclude that perhaps just about everyone has a survival instinct that takes hold under dire circumstances. At the very least this was my own experience. Early on in my injured and not yet independent state, I at times had fleeting thoughts of being better off dead. While at RUSK I even sought feedback from my grandmother on how she might have felt if I had died in the accident. This was met with sobs and encouragement for me not to think of such things. It was never brought up again. When push came to shove, I wanted to stay alive at all costs.

Another brush with the afterlife came within a year's time after this, and had its origins in my burgeoning relationship with Shriners Children's Hospital. Located on the outskirts of Philadelphia, Shriners is a premier physical rehabilitation facility which leads in the research and treatment of people with spinal cord injuries. With their commitment toward quality care at no cost, the hospital attracts patients from across the country and around the globe. In fact, at the time of my first admission they were gaining wide recognition for their work in Functional Neuromuscular Stimulation (FNS), a groundbreaking concept whereby electrodes were implanted in strategic locations beneath the skin and controlled by an outer electronic unit, helping to mimic the act of walking for individuals who did not have voluntary control of such muscles. Not meant to be a cure, FNS nonetheless provided hope for those with SCI not to be solely confined to a wheelchair. Even while requiring the use of a walker for stability, it was still a better deal than what had previously been available.

Still in its infancy, the Shriners program was seeking viable candidates, which I had the potential to become. First things first, though; I had to get my body in shape. This entailed being admitted to the Philadelphia-based rehab for some serious physical therapy. It was very much needed, too, since my weight had escalated to heights never before seen. While I was never the skinniest of kids, I had really started to let myself go.

The truth of the matter was that for the longest time since the accident I was encouraged to eat a lot, for the simple reason that without the initial ability to take in solid foods, my body mass had reduced to just forty pounds. Regaining the ability to eat brought with it every child's dream: an unrestricted diet that allowed for unhealthy doses of highly fattening foods. Potato chips, ice cream, and other such treats accompanied every meal of the day. Tipping the scales in the positive direction became cause for celebration, and so I continued eating with ever increasing voraciousness. Over a period of several months my ideal weight was ultimately reached, and quickly surpassed. Like a race car driver accustomed to dizzying speeds, I soon found myself on the fast track to Blubberville.

Eating habits can be hard to change, especially when it comes to cutting down portions and choosing healthier snacks over more fattening and generally better-tasting ones. It's hard to believe I didn't eventually pick up on my own the need to lose weight. You'd think I would have gotten the hint when my mom started wearing a weight lifter's belt in order to transfer my fat ass to and from bed.

Being out of state for the first time at the rehab facility and not seeing at least one of my parents on a daily basis contributed to my first bout of homesickness. Alone with my thoughts, I was pretty miserable at first. Fortunately, I was kept pretty busy with a full schedule of physical and occupational therapy. It wasn't like I was stuck there, either, as I was allowed to go home every weekend.

The therapy though, oh the therapy I was made to endure. They were making me do things to which I hadn't yet been exposed. One such exercise consisted of learning how to get from my chair to the floor, and then back again. The first step in this procedure was to swing away the foot rests of my wheelchair. This was possible at that time because I had a folding, collapsible chair. With this accomplished, the idea was to then shimmy my butt to the edge of the seat and as gently as could be expected, plop down in a position of having my legs folded underneath me. While getting down wasn't as easy as might be imagined, climbing upward proved a thousand times more difficult and required a whole lot more assistance.

Given the degree of difficulty, I could only hope for never being required to try such an extreme transfer again. As it turned out I would get that wish, though under significantly less than desirable circumstances.

With this first and only transfer attempt occurring on a Friday, I was picked up by my parents (bless their hearts) and driven home later that afternoon. It was a very happily anticipated weekend, as that particular Saturday was the only time Maria ever visited our home. Unfortunately, I woke up that day feeling just lousy with some congestion and a somewhat swollen right leg. My illness became progressively worse throughout the day, regrettably leading to Maria being brought home earlier than scheduled. By Sunday morning, the condition of my leg had not improved and I was beginning to experience some difficulty breathing, laboring to get enough air into my lungs. We made a decision to get an earlier than usual start back to Shriners.

It was a wise choice, too, as upon my return I was quite winded. In fact, changing to a prone position only seemed to make matters worse. My sole company on the trip back, my mother did her best to provide the comfort and serenity thought best to restore a normal breathing pattern. This ultimately proved unsuccessful and before long, I was placed on oxygen. With it came some much appreciated relief, though only temporary in nature.

Not a hospital equipped to handle conditions of an intensive nature, it was deemed medically necessary to have me transferred to a facility located more toward Philadelphia's inner city, called St. Christopher's Hospital. Following a series of tests, I was diagnosed with pneumonia. Furthermore, an x-ray revealed a break of my right femur, the sure result of that awkward floor transfer some forty-eight hours prior.

Back in an intensive care unit, the steady stream of provided oxygen was becoming increasingly ineffective. From my vantage point among the ward of beds I could see my mom speaking with the physician and nurses at their central station. As she walked back toward me, I sensed she was not about to deliver the happiest of news. In fact, the game plan was for me to be sedated and placed on a respirator. This was quite an upsetting pill to swallow. The protests I voiced were to no avail. Being hooked up to an artificial breathing machine would allow treatments to be administered with me in a more restful state.

I later awoke to the news that my father was on his way after his evening shift of work at Entenmann's Bakery. Having both of my parents present would provide a welcome measure of comfort. Sick as I had become, the recovery process was slow and extended over the course of several days. It was quite depressing just to be lying there for so long. My attitude deteriorated to such an extent that thoughts took hold of not wanting to live any longer if my future held in store more such incidents of hospitalization. The final straw came when my mom was beside me, looking at herself in a compact mirror. Curious as to what I looked like intubated, I implored her through hand gestures to hold the mirror up to my face.

The sight beheld was horrific to my eyes. Looking away immediately, I began to cry. At that moment I made up my mind that I'd had enough. I wanted so badly to throw in the towel, tired of fighting when only bad things seemed to happen.

From a medical standpoint, the timing for this new-found philosophy couldn't have been worse. I was by no means out of the woods and could really have used all the help I could get in trying to make a full recovery. This included the will to fight against my illness, something that was quickly waning. Unknown to me at the time, even the doctors were expressing doubts of my making it through.

It was again my parents, especially my dad, who provided the much needed kick in the ass to get me out of my doldrums. In a "circle the wagons" type of speech, I was reminded that as a Hawkins I was not made to give up under any circumstances. It was also emphasized rather strongly that I had already come too far to turn back now. Producing its desired effect, the speech worked like a charm, as from that point I gathered the strength to overcome yet another life challenge.

The lesson I take from this experience is that we all need people in our lives to help us through times when it just doesn't seem worth the effort to carry on. Let's face it, you don't have to have a debilitating injury to realize that life is hard. Sometimes just getting through the day under normal circumstances can be a chore. Any added chaos or stress can contribute toward throwing one's hands in the air. Who, for instance, has not experienced a loss of some sort that brings with it feelings of depression, anger, or some other negative emotional state? With this in mind, it's imperative not to discount the impact of a positive support network. If you as the reader have such a network in your life, be eternally grateful. The best friend one can have is someone who'll both provide needed comfort on one hand but will also call you out on the carpet when appropriate. If you should survey the landscape of your social contacts and recognize the absence of such influences, go out and obtain some. Join a club, or perhaps seek reconciliation with a long lost friend or family member. You will surely be a happier, more mentally sound person for doing so.

As an aside, I never did have an opportunity to participate in the FNS program. Ultimately, it proved to have its own set of problems. In fact, I was saddened to witness a most severe negative side effect. Also a patient at Shriners, Karen Bialek had the same type of injury as mine except in a lower region of the spinal cord. Karen was as sweet as could be, displaying compassion and humility not often seen among the teenaged youth around her. She hailed from New Jersey, and up until we fell out of touch many years later I considered her a close and dear friend. The major problem she and others encountered was the proliferation of infection occurring at the various implant sites. I remember Karen becoming very ill as a result and requiring additional surgeries for the electrodes to be properly removed.

As if these two weren't enough, there would be a third (and to this point, final) post-accident near-death experience. It was drug-induced and occurred in my senior year of college at Stony Brook University. Not so easy to admit, during this particular time I acquired a habit of smoking marijuana. In all honesty, my pattern of use increased to a zenith of smoking at least three times per week.

It was the perfect set up. Living on campus, I shared a suite with four other students. Within the suite were three rooms and a small kitchen shared among us. There were two students per room, except for my own privately occupied abode. Three of my suite mates from the previous year had graduated, making room for new students. One of those happened to be another senior named Avery, an average guitar player and humanities major with whom I immediately clicked. He turned out to be a habitual pot smoker with an on-campus connection that could be regularly relied upon.

Avery and I usually spent our time together in his suite, sharing some deep conversation while enjoying mixed drinks of Southern Comfort and Coke. As we grew closer, he eventually pulled out his stash of grass and I joined him, after a brief and not very convincing hesitation, in the sharing of a single joint. Not that I hadn't gotten high before, as during my first two years of college I was introduced to the drug and used it on the handful of occasions it was made available to me. By no means had I been hooked, nor did I have any intention of smoking again prior to meeting Avery.

After that first time with him I didn't expect that developing a regular drug habit was on my horizon. But that's exactly what happened. With increasing regularity I invited myself to Avery's room when his roommate was sure to be away for some time. There we would stay, sharing a joint between us and talking nonsense about one subject or another. I enjoyed the experience of being high. That feeling of being outside myself and without a care in the world was quite pleasurable. Never once having asked for money in return, I think Avery was happy to have found a smoking buddy with whom to get high. It's more fun, I think, to act goofy with another participant.

Soon the progression of use so closely associated with active addiction began to take hold, so that we were eventually smoking at a pace of at least three days per week. What used to be regulated to the weekends now bled into school days and evenings, basically whenever the opportunity presented itself. The amount of marijuana being smoked and the method of inhalation also changed. Instead of one joint we would share perhaps two, then maybe we'd say the hell with rolling a bone and let's just light up from a bong instead. On this pattern went until the approaching end of the fall semester. Then came a cold, dark day, in early December of that year, 1996.

Semester's end was always associated with a great deal of stress. Between final exams and lengthy term papers to write, my nerves at this time were always on edge. This was largely due to self-imposed pressures that presented themselves in the form of preparation overkill. In the midst of one of these academic meltdowns I was happily invited to an extended smoke session, with Avery having returned to the suite with a large quantity of product on his hands. We proceeded to get absolutely ripped, more so than on any previous occasion. Avery definitely outdid himself by scoring some seriously good shit. There we stayed in his room, passing joint upon joint between us. Perhaps three were shared in total. As if that wasn't enough (and believe me it was), Avery's bong soon made an appearance. Severely losing touch with reality led to complete uncertainty regarding the number of hits ultimately taken. Needless to say, a very large quantity of marijuana was sucked deep into our lungs.

It must be mentioned that I'm somewhat of a lightweight. Although not among the strongest of muscle relaxants, the Baclofen I take to help control involuntary muscle spasms has always exacerbated the effects of alcohol on my body, so much that I achieve a significant buzz off just two beers. This same effect may help explain why, on that particular afternoon, I was close to becoming among the first people to die from complications of cannabis inhalation.

It hit me rather suddenly. One minute I was having a grand old time talking all kinds of gibberish while bopping away to James Brown singing "Sex Machine." Almost as quickly the room began to spin in dramatic fashion. It took all sorts of effort just to make my way over to a bit of desk space before completely passing out. Leaning over with my head on the table, I proceeded to drift in and out of consciousness without any form of muscle control. Barely audible, Avery's faint voice could be deciphered with offerings of encouragement to just take it easy and go with the experience. All the while I was seriously tripping, so much so that, like a brownout, I could feel my brain going on shut down. My concern grew about my inability to communicate and otherwise manipulate the immediate environment.

The next sensation I became aware of was drifting toward a bright light that I took to symbolize death. I was convinced I was heading toward a state of nonexistence and there appeared to be nothing I could do about it. I envisioned a near future that consisted of my parents weeping over my dead form, lamenting over not having seen me graduate college and fulfill my potential. Avery was finally catching on to my plight as he began to sternly inquire about my need for assistance. Sensing his beginning to panic, as well as my own dilemma of staving off the ever approaching bright light of death, I gathered every available ounce of resolve and sat back up in my chair. Let's just say I never saw a room spin so much in my life. Somehow I managed to get the point across that I was okay (yeah, right!) and then proceeded out of Avery's room and down the ten feet or so of hall space to my own dwelling.

As I went, I had an overwhelming sense of tiredness and being incredibly cold. What I wanted more than anything was to get into bed and under complete cover of my

112

electric blanket. Remaining severely impaired and out of touch with reality, I associated doing so with lying in my own coffin, from which there would be no return. Faced with an uncomfortable chill, I decided to lay myself down anyway. Here I was still under the impression that to do so meant never again to awaken.

From this standpoint you might imagine the feeling of relief to have opened my eyes after sleeping for what seemed like days. In actuality the time elapsed was less than three whole hours. Nevertheless, with a somewhat clearer head, I was overcome with gratitude for actually being alive. There was renewed excitement about the opportunity to fulfill life's goals. And though it did not coincide with being the happiest time of my life, I was at least refocused on the accomplishment of obtaining a college degree.

Admittedly it's up for serious debate whether my life was really in danger, or if the marijuana was perhaps laced with some sort of hallucinogen. Whatever the case, I learned a valuable lesson from this at least perceived near death experience: always to be aware of what it will ultimately mean to have lived a satisfactory existence. To this end, I try to live my life by one simple rule. Namely, if I were to die at this very instant, I'd like to do so with as few regrets as possible. This entails a careful assessment of goals wanting to be accomplished and being actively involved in the process of their fulfillment. Proper decision making is of prime importance, by thinking behaviors through to all potential consequences before acting. Such practice may go a long way toward helping ensure being able to look back upon a fulfilling life span, instead of being left scratching and clawing for one more day that may no longer be available.

Since that marathon session I have not smoked or used marijuana in any other way. It was offered to me plenty of times after that point also, you can believe that. My resistance was due mostly to firsthand knowledge of what the drug was capable of. Avery went on with his habit, which managed to cause something of a wedge in our relationship. While vowing to remain in touch following graduation, we procrastinated in our exchange of phone numbers and ended up not seeing each other on the day of final ceremonies.

Looking back, it was probably just as well. Maintaining communication with the one person I most associated with drug use made the potential too great for giving into urges and reverting to old behavior patterns. There I go, sounding like the substance abuse counselor I once was. With the lack of self-disclosure often warranted by counselors in the therapeutic setting, it would be interesting to gauge the reaction of a former client gaining the information just provided.

CHAPTER NINE

Small Fish,
Huge Pond

It was in the eighth grade, three years after my back surgery, that my parents began to make some noise about mainstreaming, essentially having me return to my home school district of Sachem. Initially I was quite enthusiastic about the prospect. Number one, it meant getting away from Jay. Even after winning our fight, he still didn't leave me alone. All I heard about was the need for a rematch based on concerns that I hadn't tried hard enough to beat him. While I suppose some people are just never satisfied, truth be told, I really didn't give my best effort. I never desired to hurt Jay physically. Until the end I hoped for a reconciliation that unfortunately never happened.

The second reason for my aforementioned enthusiasm was a shortened school day due to being so close to home. No longer having to endure such lengthy travel time, I'd be returning through my front door at two in the afternoon instead of six in the evening. Unlike Sachem, Human Resources could never afford to start classes before 9 a.m. If that were the case, students living out east would be forced to wake just a few hours past midnight! Not a morning person to begin with, I wouldn't have liked that one bit.

What I thought would be another perk turned out really not to be so. Returning to my home district meant I'd be going to school again with my nearly fully-grown childhood friends. Something I had not accounted for was how different saying hi to them on the street would be from actually attending classes together. Going back to Sachem I might as well have been returning from a foreign country, as from a social standpoint I was at a major disadvantage. First, I had absolutely no roots in the daily lives of those with whom I'd be spending a third of my time. Through years of being out of the social scene, many cliques and alliances had been established. It would be difficult for most teenagers to drop in out of nowhere and join the ranks of a very closed system. Combine this with the outsider in question being in a wheelchair and what you have is a recipe for disaster. Also, it did not help matters that out of two thousand students I was the only one with such a serious disability. Talk about culture shock! Of course, it's not that I hadn't been around able-bodied people since my accident. I had not, however, been exposed to so many and in such a concentrated space.

The age group by which I found myself surrounded did not exactly help, either. Again, as the old saying goes, kids can be cruel. While that may certainly be the case, teenagers can be downright ruthless. This played itself out on my very first day of the ninth grade. To say I was shunned by my school aged peers is not an overstatement. In fact, I don't remember a single word being spoken to me outside of a teacher's voice. God forbid someone chose to sit next to me either. One of my classes, the first one in fact, took place in a sectioned-off part of the cafeteria. It was the type of deal where the walls slid along tracks in the ceiling and could be closed off to help create a classroom atmosphere. For seating, the long cafeteria tables were utilized with their attached benches. Three rows of three tables each were set up in this manner, more than accommodating the roughly thirty students in attendance. Allowing for extra time to find my way, I was seated and ready to go a little early. To be fair, I also didn't have the added distraction of meeting up with friends in the hallway before class.

In order to take advantage of any semblance of desk space, I was forced to situate myself at the far end of the rows of tables. Feeling nervous and a bit timid, of the three options open to me I chose to park in the back corner of the makeshift room. Wouldn't you know that as the rest of the students of this early morning English class filed in, not one of them sat at any of the last row of tables. In fact, there wasn't another body within a good twenty feet of me. To that point in my life I don't remember feeling any more isolated. I could tell right then I had a long four years ahead of me.

Other problems abounded. Near the top of the list was the fact that there was no elevator in the building. To say the least, this complicated my need to access the upstairs classrooms. As a "solution," at least once a day I trekked outside and had to be assisted up a huge hill toward an alternative entrance. This was true even in the coldest winter months. At times the trip was downright treacherous, especially in the event of heavy rains. The buildup of water had the effect of camouflaging a rather severe lip that existed on either side of the hill's concrete base. As the setup may imply, such conditions led to my taking a large slip one day and I became completely soaked. Luckily, that was the extent of the suffered indignity. No broken bones or other such injuries were incurred.

Despite such challenges, one thing I was determined to make sure of is that my grades would not suffer. I at least had the opportunity to excel in this area, which could serve as a bridge toward the development of friendships. I desperately needed a hook and, the way I saw it, it was better to fit in with the smart kids than with no one at all. My determination to succeed on the academic front was also spurred by a rather insensitive remark by my father, one that only from the writing of this book does he have any knowledge I overheard.

Backing up a bit, I always had a history of doing well in school. Not that it came easy to me. I had to work hard to earn favorable marks. In no way, shape, or form could I just show up on test day without proper preparation and expect to succeed. Though who wouldn't want to be one of those latter types of students? They were always envied, those peers who could simply roll out of bed with total ignorance and still not score anything lower than a B-. Now in my more advanced age, I'm not sure they had it so good. It's my feeling that there are long term merits to dealing with such a challenge as academic adversity from a young age. It helps set the foundation for personal character that does not easily succumb to later challenges.

From a young age I was provided with the structure crucial for my academic success, as time was set aside each day after school for the completion of homework. As begrudgingly as I adhered to these conditions, it's nevertheless a practice I plan to pass on to my own children someday. The sense of Mom and Dad being invested in my education was confirmed in later years, when it was expressed how they wanted to bestow upon me the opportunity to receive a higher level of learning then they had been able to achieve. At that point in time they each had no more than a high school diploma.

While a student at Human Resources I performed so well in the classroom as to earn valedictorian honors for my elementary and junior high school classes. This was a big deal as each entailed presenting a speech at the time of graduation to an auditorium filled with parents, teachers, and fellow students. The speech I recited following the completion of sixth grade did not go off without a serious hitch. Sitting on stage with the worst kind of cotton mouth, the microphone helping to carry my nasally voice suddenly went dead. Only halfway through with my presentation, with nerves frayed like ripped denim, I had no idea how to respond. It was one of those moments when you wished to crawl in a hole or be swallowed by the earth. After what seemed like a very long time (in reality it was probably just a single minute), I turned my attention to the school adminis-trators, also seated on stage. Following a few odd crack-les of static, the unit was replaced and I was able to proceed. Afterwards I received many compliments on how calm I appeared through all that chaos. In no way was I as poised as other people's impressions. It goes to show how true it can be that a person may not look as nervous as they are.

Wanting to leave Human Resources School on a high note, I worked tremendously hard to be at the head of my junior high class. Among such a small sampling of students there were only a few other realistic candidates, one of whom was my old buddy Jay. I remember thinking at the time just how sweet it would be to beat him out of this opportunity. Talk about the perfect going away pre-sent!

With this in mind, I really buckled down and put my nose in the books. Seemingly always the case, my hard work paid off. The third quarter grades were finally in and it was time to determine the winner. Having achieved perfect grades in every subject, I got my wish. In addition to really sticking it to Jay, I was also afforded the perfect venue to express my gratitude toward the school that helped me in so many ways.

I was busting with relief and excitement having earned all those perfect marks. Anticipating heaps of praise, I couldn't wait to share the good news with my parents. My mom was the first I told. She was very happy and supportive while listening to how hard I worked to accomplish such a feat. In athletic terms, I felt I had left it all on the field and could not have worked any harder.

Now getting back to my father's aforementioned remark, I had already gone to bed before he arrived home from work that night. Having difficulty sleeping, though, I heard him come in shortly after midnight. As she sometimes did, my mom had waited up for him and was able to relay the results of my report card and what I had said about thinking I could not have worked any harder. Expecting to hear how proud he was, I strained my ears in anticipation of my dad's response. What followed took me completely off guard. Far from what I expected, in a deadpan and monotone voice my father replied that I would have to work harder to have the same success in the new school I was going to.

I was very angry when I heard this. Granted, it was not the first time my abilities had been doubted and it hasn't even come close to being the last. However, it was the source from which it came that was most bothersome, a person most counted upon as an active cheerleader toward continued progress.

Perhaps I am being a bit too harsh though. I think it can be agreed that we all at times don't articulate our thoughts the way we want them to be heard. Also, anyone could have a bad day and just be downright tired after putting in a whole day's work at a job that isn't even liked to begin with. I can't be too upset either, because the whole affair did leave me with an even stronger desire to succeed. As it turned out he was right anyway, especially given the psychological factors it would be necessary to overcome.

By far, there was no greater trial of this intestinal fortitude than what occurred three months into the start of tenth grade. The summer prior to that academic year of 1990-1991, I came across an article of particular interest in The Spinal Network, a book whose pages contained numerous resources for the community of those injured in such a manner. What had caught my attention was a segment devoted to a standing device called a "swivel walker."

The concept behind this contraption was simple enough. It had a rigid frame with a series of safety straps from chest to calves, and a plate to stand on. Motion was created by swinging one's arms from side to side, thereby creating the swivel effect for which the walker was aptly named. After receiving the support of my parents, Shriners Hospital was contacted to see if it was something they were familiar with. This turned out to be the case, and plans were soon made for me to be properly fitted.

The prospect of walking, heck, of even just standing again, had my head spinning with excitement. Even more encouraging was my ability to tolerate a vertical position via a tilt table, a motorized platform that could be raised to an ever increasing angle until being perpendicular with the ground. Positive results were also obtained from a bone density scan, which was meant to measure the degree to which I was susceptible to leg fractures. My bone mass was deemed to be within normal range and allowed for proceeding to the next step (very "punny," I know).

The proper measurements were obtained and the wait began for my customized swivel walker to be constructed. In the meantime I returned home and resumed participation in the tenth grade. Following an agonizing number of weeks I returned to Shriners on Thanksgiving weekend. It could not have come soon enough. On the ensuing three hour drive I communicated having an overwhelming sense that life was finally taking a turn toward the positive. There was a feeling of finally starting to get the breaks I believed I so richly deserved. Unfortunately, the break I did receive was altogether unwelcome.

At first, everything seemed to be going just fine. Requiring physical therapy to learn how to operate the walker, I was dropped off with an expectation of returning home in a few days. While the prospect of gaining the ability to stand on a daily basis lay before me, there was no pie in the sky idea of equating this with becoming able-bodied. However, that's not to discount the increased sense of self that would've undoubtedly been attained from feeling less disabled.

So it was that on the Monday after turkey day I had the opportunity to take my first "step" in more than six years. On the edge of a mat I sat in the hospital's physical therapy department. Then, lying down with my legs dangling underneath, I was helped into my personally-fitted walker. With straps fastened, I was brought to a standing position. The rush of blood to my head caused a brief but acute bout of dizziness. After taking a moment to become steadied, the next order of business was attempting to sway myself enough to gain actual forward movement. Being my first real try at it, some assistance was required. Move I did, though, move I did. To help commemorate the event, a long vertical mirror was held in front of me. I couldn't help but love the long-awaited sight I beheld.

Feeling I had accomplished enough for one day, I was eased back down and helped free. After transferring back to my wheelchair, I was quick to call my parents and relay the good news. Along with statements of pride and congratulations there were expressions of lament for not being able to witness the inaugural event in person. Yet it was expected they'd have ample opportunity to share in my joy soon enough. The rest of the day was mine alone, the therapists not wanting to overwork my previously dormant lower body.

As it was only midmorning, I killed some time by watching television before the arrival of lunch. A curious thing began to happen whenever I bent over or otherwise moved around. I'd get that same tingling sensation indicating the need to go to the bathroom, only a bit stronger. It wouldn't last either, just long enough for me to return to a strictly upright position in my chair. Not taking the chance of wetting myself, I went to the bathroom anyway but was not greeted with significant results. This wasn't cause for too much alarm however, as it could indicate the need to take a deuce or signify the onset of a urinary tract infection.

Throughout the day this dysreflexic signal fire picked up in intensity, so that by the time early evening came about I requested to bump up the schedule of my bowel program. It got so bad, in fact, that I couldn't bend at all without experiencing an intense tingle rushing through my skull. If I did not sit upright immediately, I felt there was a threat of passing out. Made aware of my symptoms, two nurses assisted me in a chair-to-bed transfer. Undressing revealed the source of my discomfort, and before my disheartened eyes the horror of all horrors was exposed. Just above the left knee my leg was red and swollen to twice its normal size. My heart sank to unseen depths. Like the shock of an ice cube-filled bathtub, the realization hit immediately that my leg was broken and I would never stand again for the rest of my life.

My initial reaction was not one of intense crying or yelling out as to life's unfairness. The urge to throw things in disgust was absent as well. Above all else, I was in a state of emotional shock, numb to everything including words of comfort offered by one of the nurses that I might have only suffered a sprain. I knew better. The ensuing x-ray would prove me right: a fracture to the femur undoubtedly caused by the gravitational pressures of my few small steps. I had to face the reality that years of inactivity had rendered my leg bones little stronger than a pair of toothpicks. They could no longer be counted upon to handle the application of significant weight.

This development left me crushed. Perhaps blinded by optimism, I have to admit this outcome never entered into my thinking. My dad would express that it had been one of his fears all along and that he had expected me to have taken the possibility under consideration also. I wouldn't exactly call it being naïve, either. Remember, I am pretty much a cynic at heart. In this case, though, I hadn't allowed my mind to wander in that direction. Again, for whatever reason, I came to believe my life was headed toward a totally different path, one away from the hardships to which I had grown accustomed. Wrong again.

My parents were of course contacted. Once again their lives were put on hold to tend to my misfortune. Even though neither of my parents expressed feeling this way, this notion of putting them out was something I struggled with for a great many years. In fact, it did not fully dissipate until I actually moved out on my own. Anyway, they came to the hospital the very next day and brought with them a board my dad had made to fit under my seat cushion. The wood could be turned over so that an extension protruded out on the desired side, allowing for my leg to stay immobilized in a straight position.

At least I didn't require a hard cast. Being "just" a hairline fracture, it was deemed sufficient enough to send me home with a full leg brace, worn at all times. This was the lone source of good fortune in an otherwise entirely miserable experience. Added to the psychological castration was having to face a significant decrease in my level of independence. I found myself once again needing assistance in almost all activities of daily living. These ranged from getting dressed to transferring both to and from the car and bed. Needing to exercise extreme caution in my movements, the simple act of bathing was no longer a solely independent enterprise. As a teenager, few things are more embarrassing than being seen naked by your own mother. The feeling of such an experience being unnatural could not be ignored. There existed a mental certainty that it was not normal and surely not occurring among the rest of my able-bodied cohort.

Speaking of which, I never felt so self conscious in my life as when I returned to school, leg brace and all. Whatever headway I had made toward social integration seemed to vanish. In most cases such progress was tenuous at best, never amounting to much more than frivolous small talk. Suddenly I felt more different than ever, acutely aware of all those staring eyes. Being no dummy, I knew what time it was, so to speak. After all, there's hardly anything looked down upon more in high school than being different from others. In order to avoid ridicule, conformity is the name of the game. At most, eccentricities are only tolerated if the person possesses a remarkable skill or attribute such as athletic prowess or exceptional beauty. So I'd cry myself to sleep at night, hoping upon hope that morning would not arrive and I'd avoid another day on display like some side show freak.

Looking back, I think there were a few other factors at work that made for a very limited social experience throughout my high school career. First, I believe the mere sight of me represented a vulnerability no ordinary teenager likes to acknowledge (Are they even capable, I wonder?). Especially prevalent in this stage of life is an air of invincibility, a sense of being impervious to sustaining considerable physical misfortune. If only on a subconscious level, I believe the isolation I experienced was based largely on my peers not wanting to consider that I wasn't so different from them, that their own lives could just as easily change at a moment's notice.

Even against this backdrop, I think I'd have been able to secure an increased number of friends by displaying a more dynamic personality. Fully demonstrated in my attitude and behavior, I made little attempt at dispelling the image of a handicapped person through initiating positive conversation among my peers. Not liking myself left me feeling devoid of anything to offer that was of my own giving. The few students with whom I did form school-based social relationships were those who took a chance and reached out to me.

Not that I didn't try at all, despite the obstacles previously described. This showed itself through a swift shunning of the adaptive services made available by school administration. In particular, it was offered that an aide provide accompaniment to each of my classes. Their duties included carrying my books, helping to manipulate my locker, and making sure I wasn't trampled in the hallway when classes were let out. Having an adult constantly by my side created the same effect as if surrounded on all sides by a ten foot fence. *Nobody* talked to me. Despite the imposed inconvenience, after the first week of freshman year I opted against the further use of an assisting companion.

Getting right down to the truth, my miserable high school experience can be summed up in this one maxim: perception is reality. Put another way, thought will dictate behavior. Wanting to be anybody else but myself glowed like a bright sun through rays of timidity and social awkwardness. In any type of study group or class project I could be counted on for the least amount of verbal participation. And on the rare occasion of being engaged in a conversation, I had a notion to turn my head and see who was *really* being addressed.

Relegated for the most part to my own little world, it was an eye-opening experience to read the comments of those agreeable to signing my 12th grade yearbook. There are two writings that particularly stand out. One of them reads:

> *Dear Derek, I've known you forever. I am so sorry we lost touch. You're a special person. I know you'll accomplish all of your goals. I can't believe we're graduating, it seems like only yesterday that we were 7 years old. Time plays true tricks I guess. Dare to dream because your dreams will become a reality one day. Always remember the memories, and always stay sweet.*

In what may be an even greater indictment against my personality at the time, another student wrote "Remember soccer and all the special times. You're a great and brave person." With their references to the past, both messages chronicle where my head was at the time. Each invokes a sad connotation that I've grown to find increasingly disheartening.

Through this learning experience of monumental proportions, I was able to see with greater clarity the role I played in promoting how I was seen. It was a bitter yet necessary pill to swallow in order to take more risks and break out of my shell. In the end, I've come away feeling it is the responsibility of the individual to take control, to the fullest extent possible, of how they are perceived. Put perhaps in simpler terms, the impression I make upon others is largely up to me.

Happily, I can announce that through it all I was able to keep the self-made commitment of achieving good grades. While unable to sustain my streak as consecutive valedictorian, I was able to finish in the top ten percent of my 1993 graduating class. Overall my grades were good enough to secure membership into the

National Honor Society, an accomplishment worthy of pride if I do say so myself. Let this serve to illustrate a central truism of that which makes me tick. Namely, when posed with life's challenges I will either overcome them or die trying.

CHAPTER TEN

The "C" Word

Planning for college attendance was on the minds of many Sachem High School seniors, including me, during the 1992-93 academic year. Anticipating all that is associated with the college experience, I would say that the predominant mood displayed among my cohort was a mixture of anxiousness and excitement. This seemed to be particularly true for those seizing the opportunity of going away to school. Finally relieved from direct parental observation meant gaining the space needed to find oneself.

Of course at age 17 or 18 it was hardly articulated as such. A poll would almost assuredly indicate that the most anticipated feature was participation in the party life. Consciously or not, students looked forward to a whole lot of fun to be had before entrance into the real world with its emphasis on 9 to 5 employment and settling down with a partner of choice. In this particular manner, college may be seen as the bridge to adulthood.

For me, though, absolute dread would most accurately describe my thoughts on attending post-secondary education. This was especially true considering my parents' encouragement to leave home. Still without a car, I'd have to live on a college campus anyway, where bus transportation could be provided as needed. I believe also at play was their desire to afford me an opportunity that wasn't available in their own young adult lives.

The source of my dread of living on a college campus had little to do with academics and even less with concerns of homesickness. I had already addressed the latter during bouts in the hospital, and though there was sure to be an added degree of studying, I had no intention of shying away from the extra effort. Instead, my main concern was the seeming impossibility of living independently.

At home I was still utilizing a hospital bed and it remained difficult at times to clean myself following the occasional messy bowel accident. I saw no solution for the making of my own bed, nor, with the washer in the basement, had I ever done a load of laundry. For mostly these reasons I had considered it a dodged bullet having left Human Resources School before the twelfth grade. There, tradition dictated that for an extended weekend, seniors lived among themselves at a housing complex attached to school grounds.

Sulk as I might, there was no avoiding the fact that I'd have to live away from home. Following an exhaustive search that included a visit to North Carolina, the school we finally settled upon was Hofstra University. Hofstra was an attractive choice for a number of reasons. For instance, there was the quality of being out on my own while not so far from home. Located in the town of Hempstead on Long Island, it was an approximately forty-five minute car ride. Another bonus was its long-standing reputation as being user-friendly for people with disabilities. My grandfather was always fond of relating how he attended the same university many decades prior, and how it had been curious to witness gaps deliberately worked into vast stretches of concrete curbing. It was the first he knew of any private institution implementing curb cuts.

Officially, I applied to Hofstra only after breaking the score of a thousand on my SAT's. Listed as a prerequisite for admission, finally obtaining a 1060 after three attempts stands as a testament to the trouble I've always experienced with standardized tests. Following the waiting game that commences upon submission of all relevant materials, statements of pride were showered down on me after receipt of an acceptance letter.

Being surrounded by expressions of happiness did little to assuage my ongoing nervousness. Limited relief did arrive after securing the services of a legally blind student aide. Sympathetic to the needs of others, he possessed the brawn necessary to help assist in all aspects of physical maneuvering.

As it turned out, he was never utilized. Necessity being the mother of all invention, I was able to come up with ways to, among other things, make my own bed and do my own laundry. And though I cannot remember the name of that blind student aide, I was nevertheless appreciative of his availability and willingness to help others.

This brings me to a worthwhile mention. First, humor me if you will, reader, by playing a little game of word association. What I'd like is for you to conjure up as many images as possible regarding the word "cripple." Okay, so what did you come up with? Chances are those images denoted frailty and weakness. After all, the word cripple carries with it a wholly negative connotation. It is a label I absolutely cannot stand, one as bothersome to me as hearing a black person referred to as the "n" word.

Just as some African Americans have, though, people with disabilities have claimed this derogatory label. Like the "n" word, "cripple" is an acceptable term of endearment when used among members of this select group. Otherwise it must be considered off limits. Unfortunately, my best friend, who himself has a traumatic brain injury, tends to be a bit too liberal in applying this description to me in public. The stares evoked are a source of embarrassment for which I've playfully yelled at him on a number of occasions.

While I do altogether loathe the term, it is sad to say there are those among the community of people with disabilities whom it fits. This point is especially brought home on those occasions when I encounter a former peer from Human Resources School at venues such as the mall. Those cripples I speak of are invariably overweight and disheveled in their appearance. With a wardrobe that might consist of undersized sweatpants or some other bum-around Sunday clothing, they are even more apt to be perceived by the able-bodied as people to be pitied or otherwise looked down upon. Then there's the smell! Nothing quite screams inferiority like a bad case of body odor or a full diaper. Either through being enabled, giving up on life or a combination of both, these individuals occupy a segment of the disability population that can give the rest of us a bad image.

I propose that from this kind of image comes a trickle down effect. Already viewed as less than a normal person, I have experienced firsthand certain behaviors that I otherwise may not have been subjected to, behaviors that indicate a sense of entitlement among some able-bodied adults. A prime example is the uninvited manipulation of my chair that usually takes one of two forms, either pushing or leaning on it without being granted the proper permission. Believe it or not, this absolutely constitutes an invasion of my personal space. Perhaps to add more relevance, for the able-bodied reader, consider how unkind it would be if someone spontaneously and without warning involuntarily moved you to a different spot or leaned on you like some sort of coat rack. My guess is there'd be some hell to pay.

It is also this suggested sense of entitlement that allows certain ignorant individuals to ask what is wrong with me with no qualms whatsoever. Keep in mind, this is the first question being asked of me by complete strangers. Having gained a modicum of self respect and dignity, this behavior is totally unacceptable to me, the question inarguably off limits. In fact, the last time this happened, I turned what was asked right back to that person. The expression on his face was priceless, a mixture of shock and deserved embarrassment.

Knowing what it is like to have an inferiority complex, and previously having given in to such inappropriate inquisitions, I experience a substantially positive feeling when standing up for myself. I've been through way too much to take crap from anyone. Wanting to do so for a very long time, I made the choice to embrace this liberty for all it's worth.

Though it might come across as harsh, I hereby implore all the real cripples out there to mentally rise above the experience of physical limitations. Perhaps not yet possible on a universal basis, one can at least make a decent showing in the public eye. It's true enough that the clothes don't make the man. However, taking pride in personal appearance can definitely help in feeling better about oneself. If necessary, keep repeating this mantra: Disability is not a death sentence. Unfortunately, too many lost souls maintain the converse of this statement.

From the able-bodied, I want more than anything to be treated like a regular person. In fact, I find it amazing how people with disabilities are often thought of in a dichotomous way, perceived either as incompetent morons or absolute geniuses. As is often the case with extremes, the overall truth can be found somewhere in between. Also, please consider that there is no offence taken when hearing a reference to my having "walked" into a room. It need not be quickly substituted with "rolled" or "wheeled." More than the original wording, these terms serve only to emphasize the differences between us. Finally, it must be understood that even non-crippled people with disabilities can wake up on the wrong side of the bed and have bad days, though it would seem we almost can't afford the risk of coming across as an angry cripple. Taking this into consideration, I encourage everyone, including myself, to not make snap judgments based on a single interaction.

So exactly how does one avoid becoming "a cripple of the mind?" I'd venture to say that least productive is the harboring of resentments and bitterness. Regarding the former, I have encountered those who waste time believing the world owes them something. The way I see it, nothing can be farther from the truth. In fact, as far as I'm concerned there exists a permanent debt to the universe for the opportunity of life in the first place. Upon birth there are simply no guarantees (except for death and taxes, of course). To get where you want to be takes work. It takes blood, sweat, and tears. I won't deny there's some luck involved in being in the right place at the right time. What I propose is that luck is a byproduct of hard work. Rarely does luck ever strike the idle.

I also know from experience that remaining bitter about how life hasn't progressed as planned only contributes to a state of personal misery. An illustration of my prevailing attitude as a young teenager occurred while shopping with my parents one day. Walking ahead of us at the mall was a couple with a young child of their own, who could not have been more than six years old. This kid kept turning his head around to look at me, holding his gaze for increasingly longer periods of time. Growing tired of his stares, I made the meanest face in my repertoire and shot it back at him. The payoff was to see his head whip around so fast as to lose his balance and fall to the floor, much to the consternation of his parents, who yelled at him accordingly.

My own action not counted among my proudest moments, that child's innocent behavior did not deserve to be met with such disdain. In this particular instance, my point could just have easily gotten across through a simple smile or a wave. After all, staring out of curiosity is not necessarily a bad thing. I can admit to doing so on any number of occasions. What matters most, I think, is that a person's heart is in the right place. In the case of a six year old, how could it really be otherwise?

***

In hindsight, I think it was through sheer denial that I failed to take into account the real possibility of Jay and some of my other former peers from Human Resources also being attracted toward attending college at Hofstra University. That's exactly what transpired, much to my chagrin. Unfortunately, during my freshman year we were to have one last major run in, with Jay the physical aggressor inside my very own dorm room. In this particular case, no time was wasted in bringing the incident to the school's attention. A hearing was conducted with the student council, and it was ruled that Jay not initiate any further contact with me.

So what if I tattled. The stakes had become too high, considering the policy of expulsion if caught fighting on school grounds. I refused to have my entire future jeopardized. He just wasn't worth it.

As if that weren't enough stress, there remained the area of academics to be attended to. For the first time in my life I was not receiving good marks. A notoriously slow starter, I was not immediately alarmed. Like an MVP having a slow start to his season, I had no reason to believe my grades wouldn't improve. Try as I might, there was no such turn around.

As it happened, I was actually working *too* hard. My study patterns included Friday and Saturday nights, times when I should have been out having fun. In fact it was stupid of me not to do so, especially since I had been given the right encouragement. From my father had come words of advice to work hard and play hard, speaking toward the need for balance when faced with a significant amount of stress. Throughout my first semester, the choice to not behave as such proved costly. I would finish with a 2.67 grade point average, the equivalent of a C+. While not disastrous, history dictated that I was capable of a whole lot better.

Among the changes I implemented upon returning from winter break was increased participation in extra curricular activities. With the help of my academic advisor I became involved in the university soccer team, filling a void for the volunteer position of assistant team manager. As lofty as this might sound, responsibility was limited to the keeping of team statistics. This seemed to be right up my alley, though. I've always enjoyed the manipulation of numbers and have been known to obsess a bit over the statistical indicators of my favorite professional sports teams.

To keep track of the necessary data, I was assigned to attend all of the team's home games played right on campus. There I'd be set up at a table on the sideline to record all relevant information including shots on goal and scoring summaries. Satisfying in itself, one of the more enjoyable benefits to my involvement were relationships formed within the team. In fact, there were certain team members with whom I became particularly close. Through these relationships I began to thrive socially, with invites to go out partying on weekends or gather in dorms to watch playoff hockey. These friends really came in handy when I had too much to drink and needed an escort back to the confines of my dorm room.

Toward the end of that spring semester I had a few opportunities to fill in for the manager and travel with the soccer team. The longest trip by bus was to play at Central Connecticut University. Working that game signified a turning point; the experience was no longer enjoyable. That I couldn't be as close to a game I once enjoyed so much played heavily on my mind. It became too painful witnessing the camaraderie that develops within a team, something from which I would always be separate given my physical limitations. Particularly bothersome were having to be lifted to and from the bus, and becoming privy to the locker room preparations prior to game time. Following the coach's pre-game speech, I wanted so badly to go out and play myself. From that point forward it didn't sit well that my duties were relegated to a damn clipboard.

Despite my heart no longer being in it, I persevered to the end of the season. I must have made some kind of good impression, as the position of team manager was offered to me for the following year. With a knee jerk reaction, I initially accepted the job. I ended up recanting due to personal reasons, feeding a line that it would be too difficult to fit the increased travel expectations into my academic schedule.

The last game I attended turned out to be the most memorable. Played at home, it wasn't so much the match itself as what transpired just beforehand that was important. Getting dressed that late morning, I actually bore witness to a student committing suicide. There I was, minding my own business, when my ears detected a scream, followed quickly by a blur passing my third floor window. It was one of those instances when you think to yourself "I didn't just see what I think I saw, did I?" We'd later learn that the jumper was a foreign student who was not doing well academically, something his culture would not allow. Afterwards it was impossible to go many places on campus without seeing a posted advertisement for school-based counseling services.

Personally speaking, I don't judge anyone for committing suicide and would hope that those having done so aren't subject to eternal damnation. I clearly see how it can be viewed as the only means of escaping a miserable existence. To be sure, many times I have contemplated taking my own life. On those occasions of feeling I've had enough ("fuck the world, I want to get off," as a good friend of mine would say), the most imagined method is a kitchen knife to the belly when no one's home to stop me. Fear of not doing the job correctly has always kept me from following through.

On especially stressful days the thought will occur to me that being dead and not having to worry about life any longer is an attractive proposition. What stops these thoughts from gathering speed is a reminder that this option will always be available and that things haven't necessarily gotten *that* bad yet. So I end up putting it off for another day, believing I still have a lot yet to accomplish. As Fred Dryer in one of my favorite television series, *Hunter*, would say, "It works for me."

CHAPTER ELEVEN

True Companion

Prone to an attraction toward olive skinned girls, my choice of wife was the complete opposite of a partner with whom I could see myself living. With a rather frumpy appearance at the time of our first acquaintance, she had straggly blond hair that was fairly unkempt, unremarkable blue eyes, and the fairest skin you could ever imagine.

We met during the summer of 1993, I a newly anointed high school graduate and she just completing the 11th grade. Geographically a half hour's drive from each other, our paths crossed due to employment circumstances.

Three years prior to that point I had begun working at a summer day camp run by the Town of Islip. I became aware of the job through my high school guidance counselor. Here was a man, Kevin Barry, who in his job went above the call of duty. Mr. Barry (or KB behind closed doors) was a ray of sunshine through those otherwise mostly dark four years. To this day we've kept in touch.

The name of the camp was T.R.R.P, short for Therapeutic Recreation and Rehabilitation Program. Though not entirely limited to this population, it was especially sensitive toward children with disabilities. In fact, this characteristic had attracted my parents toward enrolling me as a youth. Running for six weeks from July through August, each year the camp had its base at a local elementary school. In my employment there I originally started out as a true "gofer" and progressed with age to the rank of lead counselor.

The schedule of activities consisted of what you might expect: weekly field trips to local bowling alleys, beaches, and town operated pools. On site were classes in physical activity, ceramics, and other arts and crafts. In a stroke of ultimate irony, the arts and crafts teacher I had as a young camper would became my future mother-in-law.

That's right, I knew my wife's mother several years before I'd ever get to meet Heidi.

With her mother as a connection, Heidi began working at the camp in her first year of eligibility as a junior counselor. As she is fond of recounting, our future together was entirely planned out before we even said two words to each other. Seeing me from across the auditorium on her very first day, she mentioned to a mutual friend that we would become husband and wife. This was of course taken with a grain of salt, coming across at the time as the spouting of an immature girl who hadn't had so much as one previous boyfriend. In fact, I was to become the first non-relative Heidi had ever kissed.

For her it had indeed been love at first sight, an infatuation from the very beginning. Did it ever show, as from the moment of our introduction she couldn't stop talking to or about me. I knew I was in for it when at lunch one day Heidi laid out in great detail what our dream house would look like, elevator and all. This was a highly uncomfortable conversation for me to endure. The truth of the matter was that I did not share the same degree of attraction. As mentioned, I had always gravitated toward, and indeed gawked over, females with a somewhat darker complexion. Blond over blue had not historically piqued my interest.

Nevertheless, I found myself going along for the ride. After all, it was a novelty for an able-bodied female of any type to show me even the slightest attention. In the years since my departure from Human Resources School, I was zero for two in those rare occurrences of finding the words to ask someone out. Like rain after thunder, the rejections came rather immediately and left little hope for future outcomes to be much different. Thus, prom night for me was a quiet evening spent at home, depressed and no doubt angered by life's apparent injustices.

From here it's easy to see how happy I felt just to be worthy of attraction by the opposite sex. Granted, I did feel ashamed about leading her on, as it was through omission that I let the relationship get away from both of us. Almost before I knew it, we were dating. Neither of us having a car, we each had to be dropped off somewhere or required a chaperone. The latter usually fell to that aforementioned mutual friend named Kent, a fellow camp counselor some eight years our senior. Always up for a good time, he would later prove himself good company at many a college party. He of the traumatic brain injury, Kent eventually became my best man at our wedding.

The first formal date for me and Heidi occurred on August 17th, 1993. Along with Kent, we went to see *Robin Hood: Men in Tights*, a Mel Brooks film that starred a very young Dave Chappelle. I'd call it a definite must-see in the spoof film genre. Be that as it may, in what would be a common theme in our relationship, I took the initiative and reached out for her hand in the darkened theater. Again, this was a first in her sixteen years of existence. And while Heidi was easy to read as being on cloud nine, I too experienced a heady feeling at the time. Her interest in me fully cemented, we began to spend an increasing amount of time with each other.

Still, it wasn't until her self-designated "vacation from hell" that Heidi and I fixed upon ourselves the labels of "boyfriend" and "girlfriend." Just a few short days following our first date, Heidi and her family sailed on their boat to Fire Island. Speaking by phone the first night she was away, she unhappily recounted how they were mired in a miserable weather pattern that included heavy winds and torrential rain, topped off by shrill reports of thunder and lightning, never a Heidi favorite. Following another day of these conditions, I agreed to meet her for some company. Wouldn't you know, that turned out to be the lone sunny day of the entire week. It seemed a perfect sign to officially take our relationship past the friendship level.

Unfortunately, our timing coincided with the start of a new school year. I was college-bound, and it was sad to consider that our relationship would end before it really got started. The final night before move-in found a group of us watching television at her parent's house, specifically the movie *A Few Good Men* ("You can't handle the truth!"). Before departing for the evening with Kent, with his encouragement Heidi and I shared a meaningful embrace followed by an extended and heartfelt kiss. From that point we agreed to try and make things work between us. The rest, as they say, is history.

That's not to suggest there has been nothing but smooth waters along the way. For one, it was difficult for me to trust just how special a person Heidi is. After a series of events, though, even my extreme cynicism couldn't deny the fact that Heidi possessed nary a single prejudiced or mean-spirited bone in her body.

The first significant crack to my armor of skepticism occurred after we attended a Billy Joel concert. A licensed driver at last, Heidi drove us back to my dormitory, conveniently located just down the road from the venue of Nassau Veterans Memorial Coliseum. Once behind closed doors, I took the risk of changing out of my turtleneck right in front of her. What's the big deal, you might ask? Well, to that point I'd been drastically concerned about Heidi witnessing the long and unsightly scar running the entire length of my back, the prize left from my corrective scoliosis surgery.

Noting her air of innocence, I worked myself up to believe that one look at my disfigurement would send Heidi running for the hills, screaming all the while until reaching higher ground. After all, we're talking about a person who had never gotten so much as a single stitch and who'd never stepped one foot into a hospital her whole life. Bless her heart, though, she didn't even flinch. As with so many other aspects of my injury, she took my appearance in stride.

Now if that was a hurdle, then proceeding can be considered nothing less than Mount Everest. Fast forwarding to more than a year into our relationship, Heidi had miraculously secured permission to spend the night at my dorm. The understanding of her parents was that she'd sleep in a portable, makeshift bed on the floor. Yeah right! Though I have to say, it's not like we ended up doing anything of a sexual nature anyway. Truth be told, I was scared to death. This fear I speak of had everything to do with not having revealed to that point the true demarcation of my paralysis.

As far as any of my social contacts were concerned, I could feel my entire body save for my legs. Entering the age of sexual expectation, this was a safer and more socially acceptable response. I can't begin to count the number of times peers who inquired about such things would answer with, "well at least you have that." Already struggling to fit in, there seemed to be no choice but to utter the reassurance that I had full control over my bits and pieces. It is a somewhat embarrassing fact to have to report no matter what one's age. Furthermore, it wasn't expected that any of these relationships would evolve to the point of the whole truth having to be revealed.

With Heidi it was different. It was becoming increasingly clear that we were heading in that direction, albeit at a snail's pace. We *are* talking about a girl who had never before allowed the word "sex" to pass her lips. And so I was clearly the aggressor in pushing for additions to our intimacy repertoire. We started straight from the basics, too. As a prime example, I once explained to her that the next time we were together, I'd like to try a little something called "French kissing." She had absolutely no idea what I was talking about. As I got to the detail of sticking each other's tongues in our mouths, she became aghast and exclaimed, "*People actually do that*?!" Let's just say I was met with the same type of reaction on many subsequent occasions.

Getting back to the particular night of her first sleepover, I deflected all attention away from actually going to bed. There was more to it than just the prospect of sex. She was also oblivious to my lack of bladder control that required hooking myself up to a bedside drainage bag. Rather than come clean, I played it off as not being the least bit tired. To my great relief, Heidi took to the suggestion of staying up all night to talk and watch television. As the hours went by, a nagging thought grew roots that this couldn't go on forever. She was so into me. For my part, there were ever increasing feelings of guilt in not being more up front about the exact restrictions of my disability.

Again with an expectation of her leaving me, after a few days passed I laid it all out for her. Everything was revealed, including the bathroom devices I was dependent on and my inability to sustain an erection. Here was the ultimate moment of truth, my confession ending with a line similar to, "I'll understand if what I've said is a little too much to handle." "Astonishing" best describes what happened next. Heidi leaned forward to give me a great big hug. None of it mattered to her. I knew right then, beyond the shadow of a doubt, that I must have been dating an alien from outer space.

From there it might seem our relationship was destined to bloom. We did hit our stride for a while, with a growing level of comfort from having all our cards on the table. However, it was my lack of physical attraction to Heidi that eventually came back to haunt us. Almost hard to imagine now, it was up for personal debate whether I was settling for less than what I could have. I owed it to Heidi to be as completely into her as she was into me, and I simply wasn't. Part of me wondered if there was someone out there who had Heidi's personality *and* the looks I more desired.

This led to our breakup in April of 1995. I was the main culprit, presenting us as being on such different maturity levels, and pointing out that our schedules didn't allow for much time together. Heidi was emotionally crushed and would take it as her whole world ending, the love of her life slipping right through her hands. Thankfully, it was not a messy breakup; no offensive words were exchanged. Left open was the possibility of remaining friends, which is what we ought to have concentrated on from the very beginning.

This we did through the ensuing summer. There were some awkward moments along the way, as we ended up working together again at the same day camp. Being the nice person that she is, Heidi gave me a hand with rides. She'd drive me to and from work each week day. Things got touchy when conversations turned toward accusatory inquiries of why I *really* didn't want to be with her. My limited manner of answering was not received with particular satisfaction.

By camp's end, it was Heidi who initiated a desire to see less of each other in an honest attempt to get over me. The shoe was on the other foot as I was the one being put out. In all, we had absolutely no contact for more than a month.

That drought was finally broken when she called upon my assistance for a diversity paper she was writing for a summer course at Suffolk County Community College. Glad for the opportunity to help, I had written something similar in my freshman year. When she arrived at our door, it was like meeting a completely different person. She had put on a little weight (in a good way as she'd been too skinny from the time we met), plus she had gotten a very stylish haircut and, as a first, had even applied some makeup. Her updated look and manner of dress (she was wearing a tube top that showed off a flat and sexy midriff) made her appear every bit the young woman that she was. Gone was the terribly shy and reserved girl I'd known to that point. To further complicate matters, she reported being unable to stay for dinner due to having a date. A date!! I could not believe my ears. Suddenly, I was experiencing feelings of jealousy that I hadn't thought possible when it came to Heidi.

It was through this transformation that I began to see her in a completely new light. With a good degree of soul searching, I reached the conclusion that it was personality type that drew my attraction more than anything else. In this respect I did a bit of growing up myself, as besides her newly developed physical looks, I was especially drawn to her new air of confidence and self assuredness.

That being said, knowing how badly I had already hurt her led to an exercise in caution by not whimsically seeking to reenter an intimate relationship. In hindsight it was a good thing, too, as more time was required for us to sort things out individually. Albeit in its infancy, the foundation for the future success of our life together was taking form, with Heidi's realization of not needing to be with me to survive, and my own that I wanted her firmly in my life.

CHAPTER TWELVE

The Calling

In the fall I returned to school, albeit to a different university. Following that second year at Hofstra, I decided to transfer to SUNY at Stony Brook, a state-run school located in Suffolk County and therefore much closer to home. Still without a car, I again took full advantage of on-site housing. By that time I came to thoroughly enjoy being on my own and would have considered it a step backwards to live with my parents again on a full-time basis.

As do many things in life, the change in schools had much to do with financial considerations. In the midst of trying to achieve Ivy League status, Hofstra's tuition was rising to astronomical levels. There was an increase of about six thousand dollars from my first to third year's bill. As renowned as it was for the accommodations made toward people with disabilities, you have to draw the line somewhere. This is especially true if not blessed (as I wasn't) with at least a partial scholarship.

While usually not fearful of change, I was leery about this. My main concern was for the quality of education I would be receiving. Already I surmised that significantly lowered fees would equate to less in the way of learning. However, the anticipated deficiency never came to fruition. In fact, I found Stony Brook to be more education-focused than Hofstra had been. Generally speaking, it appeared that each school served a different population, with more SUNY students paying their own way than did Hofstra students. In this case the overall disparity in educational investment is understandable, as when paying for something it tends to mean more and is therefore taken more seriously. No matter what it might be, I think we would all like something to show for the money we spend instead of just pissing it away.

One negative aspect of the change had to do with the school's physical infrastructure. For my purposes, the campus was definitely not user-friendly. There were more hills to navigate and the buildings were spread apart. Still, I managed on my own even through the cold winter months. So it took a greater effort and a little longer to get places. To me the greatest priority was keeping my independence.

Save for helping me to move in, most of the contact between me and Heidi was relegated to the phone. Despite my renewed interest I tried to move on from her as well, confused by my emotions into thinking that staying apart was perhaps for the best. She appeared to be having a much easier time of it, although that one date of hers hadn't developed into anything serious. Still, she gave no indication of being desperate to get back with me. I was without many prospects myself, though there was one girl living in the same building with whom I became friendly. We were both elected members of the Roth Quad Council, a group of students who met periodically to set certain rules and schedule events within our residence. More than anything, it was a way to add another item to my resume of extracurricular activities. Anyway, this attractive girl did agree to have dinner with me at a time to be determined. But before this date occurred, Heidi and I agreed to get back together.

It started with a phone call that ended with me inviting Heidi to come over. As late as it was that night, I was surprised she said yes. Accept the offer she did, though, and when she arrived I couldn't help but notice a charge from within me that signified physical attraction. For the first time since we met, I truly wanted her. It was a want not for the moment but for the long haul. With the personality and looks to match, Heidi had become the person with whom I could see spending the rest of my life.

The circumstance had finally arrived that would allow us once again to become a couple. What was supposed to be a simple goodbye, I encouraged Heidi to consider that one rather innocent kiss wouldn't hurt before parting for the night. That simple peck turned out to be an elongated "make out" session. Our talk that followed led to a number of excited calls placed to family and friends, informing them we were back together. From then on there have been no further breakups or other such separations of the heart.

Come that spring season, having finished up my junior year in undergraduate studies, it was time to put some serious thought into what I wanted to do for a career. One thing I did know for sure: from as far back as I could remember, I had as my primary vocational goal the desire to help people. Not surprising, since generally speaking I enjoy giving of myself to others. Taken to an even deeper level, becoming part of the helping business would allow me to honor those professionals who helped me along the road of recovery.

Throughout my educational journey this desire took on various forms. At first, my sights were set on becoming a lawyer. Here I had a positive role model in my Uncle Danny (on my mother's side), to whom I've always looked up and who is an attorney of many years with his own practice in Arlington, Virginia. For my own niche, I considered specializing in disability advocacy. This way I could fight against the violation of rights and other injustices brought upon my disabled peers.

Whatever plans I had were quickly dashed upon entering college and taking the first in a series of required political science classes, commensurate with a chosen major of the same name. I found these courses to be altogether too dry and boring. In fact, I had such a difficult time staying awake that it wasn't uncommon to find the desk holding my head up. Realizing rather quickly that law was not the work I was destined for, I then switched to the most common of university majors, that of liberal arts. Seeing that the course catalog was designed for those not having a clue what to do with their lives, I decided to broaden my horizons when it came time to select my courses.

With this in mind, I enrolled in Introduction to Psychology. From there, I was hooked. I found it fascinating to learn how the mind works, including the various factors that help shape one's personality and overall ways of thinking. The catalyst had been provided, which led to settling on the psychology major I'd carry throughout my remaining undergraduate career.

Fast forwarding to the anticipation of my senior year, it was time to start figuring out the concentration I would pursue in graduate school, made necessary by the fact that there are none too many jobs out there for the holder of a B. A. in psychology. In the same regard, a profound decision-making influence was my growing weariness of attending school altogether. So while I first set my sights on becoming a psychologist, taking this route would have meant adding another four years to my academic career, as earning a decent wage in the field of psychology required no less than a doctorate. Honestly speaking, I was not prepared to work that hard for so long. Searching for a suitable alternative, my attention was drawn toward Stony Brook's School of Social Welfare. Here was a two-year program that allowed for the obtaining of a master's degree in social work. While the option would always be open to go further, the benefit of becoming Dr. Hawkins in this field rested solely in being able to teach as a professor. Not seeing myself ever again setting foot in a classroom, I didn't anticipate this becoming an issue.

Now that I had settled on a field of study, the crucial decision of which schools to apply to was imminent. In the end, three universities made the cut: Stony Brook, Adelphi, and Rutgers. The first two being local, The State University of New Jersey at Rutgers was located quite a driver's distance from home. From the start this was Heidi's least favorite option. I wasn't too enamored of it either, save for its reputation as one of the leading social work programs in the entire nation. I had my own qualms about spending the better part of two years in a neighboring state, the least of which concerned having no idea as to the navigational landscape. For as my wife is glad to reveal, and which I can not readily dispute, I'd have a hard time finding my way out of a paper bag.

Instead, at the summit of my list of hesitations was the anticipated lack of regular physical contact with Heidi. We were doing so well together that it seemed a real risk to change in any way the dynamic of our relationship. On the other hand, the increased time apart from each other could serve as the final barometer of whether we were meant to last. In the end, it was the latter that proved correct.

So although I received letters of acceptance from all three of these schools, I ultimately chose Rutgers. By attending the more reputable school I hoped to increase my marketability when it came time for graduation and the big job search.

The rest of that summer was somewhat trying, Heidi remaining none too happy with me for what she saw as my leaving her, as if we weren't going to see each other again for an entire year or something. Granted, if I had to do it all over again I think I'd have made an alternative decision and stayed local, since going to Rutgers has not appeared to provide a significant advantage. During interviews, I never had the impression that the Rutgers name jumped off the page to potential employers.

My last night home was particularly difficult. I had been in a horrible mood for some time, and as was my wont, upon inquiries from my parents about what was the matter, I wouldn't budge, choosing instead to continuously respond with a meek "nothing." By that late hour I also hadn't assured the proper arrangements for my pending arrival at college. As huge as it was, in order to navigate Rutgers' campus I would require the aid of university-sponsored handicapped transportation. (These were the adaptive mini buses I'd initially rely on to get to and from my scheduled classes. Without effective coordination, I was sure to be up the proverbial shit creek without a paddle. Although arranged hastily and not without complication, luckily the transportation support was set up when I got there.)

No longer allowing me to stop at "nothing," my parents pushed for a more articulate answer. I can't say they got what they wanted initially because I burst out in tears. The major source of my lament was that I was going to miss Heidi. In the simplest of terms, I was crying over a girl. Let the teasing begin, as like Niagara Falls I expected the floodgates to open. Instead, I received an abundance of much needed support. I imagine there was relief on the part of my parents to have finally been let in and told the truth.

Still concerned, but at least feeling a little better, with the company of Heidi and my parents I was brought the next day to greet my brave new world. Or "Pee Wee's Big Adventure," as my dad would say to help lighten the mood.

How different it was, too. I know I must have had that "deer in the headlights" look for quite some time. The aesthetics of New Jersey was a great surprise, as I erroneously imagined an oil refinery within every few square miles. There was also a feeling of being out on my own more than at any other time. The adjustment hit me hard, to the point of not wanting to stay after just the first week or so. In fact, I called my father on his statement that if going to school in another state wasn't working out, then I'd be able to come home. His response was that I hadn't given it enough time. Something tells me, though, that no matter how much time and opportunity I provided there would've always been a reason for me having to stay.

Faced with this unsettling reality I was able to tough it out, however begrudgingly. In all honesty, I gained a bit of perspective from one of my suite mates at the time, named Ahmadu (I am no doubt butchering the spelling of his name). Here was a guy whose wife and child lived in his African homeland while he pursued a better education in America. Internalizing his story made it easier to consider how my own separation from loved ones wasn't nearly as profound.

Nevertheless, how I longed for those visits from my woman! My conjugal visits of sorts would occur about once a month on the weekend. Heidi would take the train, a circuitous route that included a transfer at Penn Station. There was my honey, as innocent as they come, having to mingle among some of the dregs of society. Ok, so I am exaggerating just a tad. Still, I'd worry sick until she arrived to me all safe and sound. God forbid the train was running late. On those occasions, yours truly was known to initiate frantic calls to her cell phone.

If I may digress for a moment, such reflection again spurs the memory of how attached I was to my parents in the early wake of my accident. Considering her role as nurturer, this was especially the case with my mom. She couldn't leave the house most times without me freaking out. If not showing on the surface, I'd enter an internal panic if she didn't return from the store or some other errand in a time frame I deemed reasonable. Worse was going with her and being left in the car while she ran into the supermarket or other such marketplace, my chair stuck in its lock. Visions of Mom being abducted or killed ran roughshod through my brain.

This emotional discomfort speaks to two issues. First, there's no concealing I was a big time momma's boy (still am I suppose, though on a more limited scale). When I needed something, my mother's the one I'd always call upon first. Not that Dad would ignore my requests for assistance, but he was far less patient in their provision.

Second, and on a more global scale, it relates back to my control issues. Even now there's a foreboding doubt and insecurity about what I could do in the event something bad happened to those closest to me. In fact, it has always been difficult to wrap my brain around a common statement by Heidi, that she feels safest when in my presence. Truth is, if someone wanted to harm her, I wouldn't stand a chance in a physical altercation.

Now getting back to those much-anticipated visits, once back at my dorm we wasted little time catching up in the way of physical intimacy. One thing I absolutely love to do is make out, which we did plenty of in those days. When presented with the opportunity, I could swap spit for hours. Sex as we knew it was pretty good as well. I was proud and embarrassed at the same time when approached by my suite mates to try and keep the noise level down when we went at it.

As the sun set on that first semester of graduate school, thoughts turned to asking for Heidi's hand in marriage. In truth, the idea hit me like a ton of bricks as the Thanksgiving holiday approached. For all our concerns about being away from each other for uncharted intervals, it was the absences that helped solidify just how special Heidi was to me. So the question became not *if* our relationship would reach the ultimate pinnacle, but when.

As is often the case with matters of the heart, the instinct was to proceed with a full head of steam. Yet while I desired to shout my intentions from the rooftops, there were other, more pressing matters at hand that required a bit of temperance. Most important was the amount of schooling still ahead for both of us. As it stood in that November of 1997, I had a year and a half before obtaining my Masters Degree. Heidi was facing a year beyond that before graduating with her own Bachelor of Arts in Recreation Therapy and Early Childhood Education.

Because money truly does make the world go around, the smart move was to tie the knot after securing jobs in our chosen fields to earn a steady income. Related to this was the matter of where we would live. Both residing with our respective parents, it seemed unimaginable to live under either of their roofs as a married couple.

Bummed to some degree that a more immediate wedding seemed out of the question, there didn't appear any harm in becoming engaged. I held onto this thought for weeks thereafter, not verbalizing my intentions to a single soul. I had long ago proved quite adept at keeping a secret. Harkening back to my father's 30th birthday in 1982, I had firsthand knowledge of his impending present, a miniature television and radio combination meant to provide accompaniment on our semiannual camping trips. Despite numerous inquiries, I held tight to the entrusted surprise. That a seven year old could keep such a tight vault was cause for much family amazement.

While home for the Christmas intersession, I finally broached the engagement plan to my parents. They were both very supportive, and as mothers can be, mine was overcome with emotion. Come to think of it, I would be too if my child announced the belief of having found their intended life partner. My parents had always gotten along well with Heidi, though they judged her as severely immature. To be fair, they also saw her genuineness and acceptance of me as a person. The latter shone through and ruled above all else. I swore them to secrecy.

The holiday season came and went. Percolating with excitement, I'd live to rue an unfortunate statement made that New Year's Eve. With all the confidence of a renowned psychic, I exclaimed to Heidi that 1998 was going to be a great year. Though I wasn't sure exactly when, my plan was to ask for Heidi's hand in marriage in the coming months.

Unfortunately my exuberance would provoke the "bad gods." Ever the pessimist, I possess the perhaps not so irrational belief that once announced, a positive thought may be stomped upon and made not to come true. So it was that 1998 had quite an auspicious start, as on January 30 I'd cause an accident while driving my first vehicle (more later on the subject of car attainment). Back in New Jersey, I did not yield nearly enough when making a right turn at a four-way traffic light. There was no arrow giving me the right of way, no excuse to offer other than that I was daydreaming. For whatever reason, that was not a rare occurrence in my early driving career. I think the simple mistakes were due to trying too hard. Overall, I became a much better driver after finally learning to relax behind the wheel.

Be that as it may, the result of my indiscretion was a badly bent rear passenger side quarter panel that rendered the van unusable. Though physically unscathed, I was an emotional wreck. It's important to note there were no injuries to the party that hit me, either. My car would eventually be fixed, but for those who know, going without it for the better part of a month was a major inconvenience.

Heidi was there for me big time as she drove out to Rutgers the very next day. Having to endure a high dose of negativity, it's a wonder she put up with me. Then again, if ask her (as I have on more than one occasion), Heidi would respond I am not someone by whom she feels put upon. She loves me to death and that's just about the greatest feeling in the world. Not realizing it at the time, Heidi was beginning to replace my parents in the way of a primary support system.

At getting my vehicle back sufficiently repaired, a sense of normalcy was welcomed with open arms. Things were beginning to look up once again, though I dared not tempt fate with any sort of swagger-laden verbalization. Yet as the eternal gloom of another northeast winter reached its conclusion, I came home and took advantage of a much needed mid-semester break. By then I figured on proposing to Heidi immediately following that spring semester. With my mind made up, it was time to get busy selecting the all important engagement ring.

Now, along with her innocence, part of Heidi's nature includes gullibility. As a prime example, she was tricked into believing that her finger needed to be measured in order for my dad to decipher the correct size when purchasing a ring for my mom. Of course this was a ruse for my own sake of gaining the information. She fell for it hook, line, and sinker. Don't ever let her say otherwise.

With the size established, the rest turned out easier than expected. First, a budget of a thousand dollars was decided upon. This was key if you ask me, as shopping with a maximum figure in mind helped to avoid the trappings of our consumer-driven society. Even so, the temptation of breaking the bank would not be an issue in this case. Possessing not a hint of pretentiousness, Heidi is far from a high-maintenance individual. In fact, she's forever reminding me of the little things that provide her with the most pleasure. Merely demonstrating that I have been thinking of her by giving her some dollar store purchase or Happy Meal toy is enough to produce a loving glow.

In the end, a simple ring was selected for a simple girl. One weird part of the whole buying experience was making the purchase at a flea market. I would never have thought to do such a thing but for the fact that my mom was referred through a friend at work. To my surprise, the very well-stocked booth had the perfect stone. It was nearly a karat and was set on a gold band with prongs extending upward on either side. As such, the diamond couldn't help but be the center of attention.

Then came the challenge of planning the proposal, both the "when" and the "how." Regarding the former, it seemed best to wait until semester's end when we'd have the most time to spend together. Providing it was a positive response (I saw no reason why it wouldn't be), I knew Heidi would want me close at every waking moment. On my side, there was also a family reunion of sorts planned for around that same time in late May. My grandmother, whom Heidi had never met, would be up from Florida. It would be the perfect opportunity to show her off and announce the big news.

As far as the "how" of the anticipated event, there was a great deal of pondering that took place, and would play itself out as follows. About a week before coming home, I called Heidi and shared my opinion of how nice it would be for us to watch a sunrise together. Now for someone like me, who's idea of early was being dressed by noon, I knew a good deal of explaining would be required. The chosen angle was to say that I was learning in class about the power of spirituality, and believed that witnessing nature's beauty would contribute toward inner peace and worldly perspective. Harboring a hint of skepticism about actually carrying this out, Heidi nonetheless agreed with the plan laid before her.

Wouldn't you know that on the arrival of the set date I would oversleep, though thankfully for just a short time. Just my luck too, at that early hour the entrance ramp of the parkway was closed for roadwork. Using my cell phone to report my impending lateness betrayed the exceedingly good mood I was in. Heidi had every right to be shocked by the happy tone of my voice. There was no reason why she shouldn't have been, given my reputation as the ultimate morning crank. I believe I won her over with assurances of happiness to be seeing her.

Upon picking her up, I navigated the two of us toward a local marina in Bay Shore, not more than twenty minutes from her parents' home. From there we would be afforded an unobstructed view of the steadily rising celestial body that is the all-magnificent sun. As early as it was, we were to have little company; those present within any kind of proximity included an oft-isolated fisherman and those just greeting the day off their docked boats.

There we sat in my car. Secured as I was in the driver's seat, I invited Heidi to trade her passenger's side captain's chair for the right side of my lap. From there I put my right arm around her waist, my left hand feeling for the decorative box of my special gift. These squirming movements were quickly called into question as Heidi requested a *full* hug. I let her down as gently as possible under the circumstances, verbalizing the excuse of being too cold and therefore needing my left hand to be pocketed for the time being.

Then I proceeded into a rather well-rehearsed speech, one that even today I can repeat with very few liberties. I told Heidi how happy I was to share nature's wonder with her. I then expressed my anticipation of it being a good day ahead, looking forward to Heidi meeting the rest of my family. And then, as I firmly gripped the box and removed my pocketed hand, I told Heidi she had to do one simple thing to make this day one of the best there ever was. Her inquiry as to what that might be was met with my response of, "Just say yes." With that, I presented the ring box before her astonished eyes.

I was feeling pretty damned good about myself in that moment, having pulled everything off as planned. That said, in the blink of an eye it all seemed to come crashing down. Like an innocent man banished unceremoniously to death row, my ears struggled mightily to comprehend her unexpected reverberation of "no, no, no." Here was the mantra I'd least expected, that's for sure. As she pushed away from me, I was relieved to gauge the expression on Heidi's face. It was filled more with stunned disbelief and delight than consternation or admonishment. As she slowly but surely regained her composure, I was pleased to be in receipt of a loving hug and a resounding "YES!"

As she soon came to explain, Heidi's initial reaction had everything to do with the timing of my proposal. Such a request wasn't expected until the following year, when I'd finish my graduate studies. I got her good, even though we were both almost shocked to death. So it all turned out well in the end, though there was one more hurdle to climb. Returning to her house, Heidi hurriedly woke her mother with the good news. From the comfort of my van's curbside vantage point I could hear the voice of my future mother-in-law stating loudly that I had not asked permission of Heidi's father. In fact, it was based on my own father's advice that I risked flouting such tradition as a relic of yesteryear. Happily, it did not become a sticking point.

CHAPTER THIRTEEN

The Great Beyond

My wife and I are opposite in so many ways that, as an outsider, I myself would wonder what in the world keeps us together. To me, the best explanation is a line from my favorite movie of all time, *Rocky*. Fielding the same question about his girlfriend, Adrian, the Italian Stallion responds simply that they fill each other's gaps. That's to say, whatever is missing from one of the couple is compensated for by the other's life experience.

It's exactly the same phenomenon that applies to the two of us. Again, with an adorable innocence, Heidi has never received a minute's worth of hospital-related treatment (knock on wood that I haven't jinxed her). She has yet to be touched by trauma in a way about which I can only dream.

In direct relation to the above, another difference that sets us apart is that Heidi had a fabulous childhood. Mind you, it isn't that she came from money and enjoyed a fairytale lifestyle. She's the oldest of three children (the other two boys), born from middle class parents who at one point shared a failed business venture leading to bankruptcy. Sheltered from its impact to the greatest extent possible, Heidi and her siblings were able to remain kids.

Of this Heidi took full advantage. If anything, she could be said to have held on a bit *too* long, as playing seriously with Barbie dolls lasted through her mid-teens. On the other hand, it is my own lost childhood that lingers as perhaps the greatest emotional pain remaining from my accident. Whereas my wife is a collector of relics from when she was a young lass, I cannot have in my grasp (or direct line of sight for that matter) anything from before my ninth birthday lest it bring lament and sadness.

Focusing on these two examples, Heidi is a good match for me in terms of keeping in check the cynicism that runs rampant due to an early introduction to life's cruel inequities. It helps being exposed to someone like Heidi, who still believes in all that life can offer and who considers goodness in people the rule rather than the exception. Having been quick to view individuals and situations through a negative prism, my own outlook on life has definitely brightened to some degree, thanks to her.

That being the case, it is duly evident that Heidi has benefited somewhat in the opposite direction, as in my eyes she has shown tremendous personal growth in drifting more toward the center, or that which is the realm of reality. Exhibit A includes her behavior and attitude toward finances. Having a healthy respect for all that can go wrong in life, I tend to be conservative in my spending habits. Thus, my purchases lean more towards needs rather than wants. It is not an unusual sight to find me staring with great intent at our account balances and family budget. With an eye on the future, I am keen on anticipating the payment of all major expenditures. Heidi, for the most part, had been devoid of such consequential thinking. All those dead presidents hardly got a chance to settle before gaining new ownership. Owing money never seemed to bother her either, whereas I'm not satisfied until all debts are paid in full.

So while at first my manner of money management was a foreign concept, along the way Heidi has adopted a more responsible approach, even if just to appease this writer's anxieties. All kidding aside, Heidi has emerged as a more diligent bill payer and saver of money. As a result, funds that might have gone to some frivolous expense have been set aside for retirement and those oh-so-unpredictable, and yet seemingly inevitable, "rainy days."

Speaking of which, I believe a byproduct of our relationship is awareness on Heidi's part that bad things do happen to good people. To me this is such an important lesson and a concept with which Heidi still does struggle. She holds close ideals such as fairness and equality. To be sure, there is no crime in doing so. However, what I suggest is that one does oneself a personal disservice by going to pieces when these expectations are not met.

With that said, there is little doubt that the greatest philosophical difference remaining between Heidi and me is our respective degree of devotion to faith and religion. Expressed in the simplest of terms, hers is abundant while my belief has never quite left the ground. In reality, the cards were stacked against me from the start. Growing up, I was hardly exposed to a religious upbringing save for the rudimentary consecrations of baptism and communion. Otherwise, I do not recall ever having attended mass with my parents. There was religion class, held within a neighbor's home in preparation of receiving the sacrament. However, the specific teachings of Christ were not reinforced and so were not deemed by this once impressionable youngster as something to be valued above all else. Learning about God appeared to be a means to an end, that end being a very stale and unappetizing wafer that tasted absolutely nothing like bread.

So my religious apathy had its roots elsewhere and was not caused by my accident. I did not suddenly denounce God at the tender age of nine. There would be plenty of time for that in later years. Questions did abound, though, as to how my accident could have been allowed to happen. Severely unequipped to handle such inquiries, I seem to remember my parents being at a loss for providing an intelligible response.

Still, an effort was sustained to forge ahead in a relationship with the Almighty. For sure, I was provided with reasons to believe. My rather vociferous prayers for the ability to walk again seemed to be answered through the format of dreams. Those at RUSK came to me as oh-so-real and awakened the hope of my physical condition being fully restored. Thanks to God it would all just be a matter of time. Needless to say, I'm still waiting.

There appeared to be even more evidence of God's existence. For example, again while at RUSK, I found myself struggling through some sleepless nights. Used to sleeping solo either at home or in a private ICU, it was hard to adjust to the almost constant noise of a shared ward. To this day I require certain conditions to get to sleep, mainly complete darkness and quiet. Yet when deep in REM, it damn near takes a nuclear explosion to wake me up. Anyway, suffering through one of those sleepless nights, I finally became fed up with staring at the ceiling. I had done enough of that out of necessity at Stony Brook to last a lifetime. Lying there frustrated and bored stiff, my attention turned to the rather nondescript, hospital-issue bedside table. The barely reachable top drawer contained my sanctuary, or so I hoped. What treasure awaited, you might wonder? Well, ever the sports enthusiast, my paternal grandfather had obtained for me a New York Metropolitans yearbook. More than anything, at that moment I craved the opportunity to leaf through its pages. Trouble was, I couldn't be sure of the magazine's exact location. And so with feverish intensity I began to pray that I might find the precious periodical.

Lo and behold, after some degree of struggle my efforts were rewarded and my prayers answered from above. From what I could tell, the existence of a benevolent God had been proven beyond the shadow of a doubt. My excitement over this fact could not be contained.

With the utmost enthusiasm I would recount the night's events to my mother when she made her daily pilgrimage. Her reply was a complete damper as she insisted my findings had nothing to do with God. Mom explained that God could not just make things appear. Accordingly, it was determined that I had not been witness to any sort of divine intervention. No doubt far from her intent, this indeed delivered a blow to my psyche.

However, nothing compares with a later occurrence that turned me totally against God and religion. The incident I speak of took place in 1988, during my second rehab stint at Shriners Hospital. I was there for corrective back surgery of a different sort than the original spinal fusion. It seems that when my rods were put in, the doctors, in their infinite wisdom, purposely left them long to allow for future growth and physical development. While perhaps a reasonable assumption, I did little of either and by my thirteenth birthday I was subject to unbearable pain on a daily basis. The rods, you see, were beginning to push their way through the skin of my upper back.

While the surgery was a success, I had yet another recovery lying before me. From my experience, there's little doubt that the immediate aftermath of an operation is the absolute worst. Almost every movement results in pain. Then there's the complete loss of independence, which I'd venture to say could send anyone over the edge into depression. My own mindset was just that. How much can a person take, I asked myself.

Alone with these thoughts, I had the television remote in hand. With no particular destination in mind, I flipped through the channels in rapid succession. Finding myself completely miserable in both body and mind, I settled upon a random station. It turned out to be a religious station with some sort of mass being performed. Normally this was not a program that would hold my interest. For whatever reason, though, I stuck with it.

The preacher, most likely an evangelist, was in the midst of a highly energetic sermon. In directing a message of healing, he called out to those experiencing physical and/or emotional pain. I couldn't help but be drawn in. To those wanting to be freed of their pain, this preacher expressed that through the Lord he could make it happen. All that was required was to believe in the power of God. The television audience was encouraged to put their hands to the screen of their sets. Lying as I was in a hospital bed, this did me no good. Hence my participation in a supposed miracle had run its course.

Or had it? Amazingly, not all was lost. In a dramatic turn of events, the preacher man beckoned to those like myself who could not reach their television screens. It would be enough, he said, to simply reach in the direction of his voice. Reach I did, just as far as my I. V.-laden hand would allow. At that point I closed my eyes as the prayer offering commenced. The opportunity to be cured of my dreadful paralysis was finally upon me. The clock was about to strike 12, only in a good way. I was thoroughly caught up in the whirlwind of manic inflections spouting from the mouth of my would-be savior.

It was over just as fast as it had begun. Yet my condition remained completely unchanged. Like the cloud cover of a rapid storm, my thoughts turned instantly. If not a full cure, I should have been given something, damn it! Some increase in sensation or the ability to voluntarily move a single toe would have sufficed. To be left in exactly the same state was absolutely crushing. Whatever degree of spirituality I possessed was extinguished. I cursed God and all his supposed power.

In recent years I've come around some, thanks mostly to Heidi. So much unlike me, Heidi grew up in the church. She is in a long line of followers, on her mother's side, of the New Apostolic faith. From my understanding and knowledge base, this religion is marked by living apostles as well as by a priesthood allowed to marry. It is progressive in this way for sure, while the message of each sermon is delivered directly from the Holy Bible.

In an effort to believe in something greater than myself I started attending church services with my wife. At first, when we were still dating, I stuck my head in exclusively on major holidays. Much to Heidi's delight, I got to meet all her church friends that had already heard a lot about me. It was on these occasions that her dad went also, a source of comfort as he too wasn't born into the faith.

Later in our marriage I made a concerted effort to attend on a more consistent basis. For about a three month period a few years ago, I went every Sunday. It didn't stick, despite my best intentions. Heck, I even followed through on meeting with an evangelist to help me better understand the central tenets of New Apostolicism. Granted, the congregation is nice enough. It's a small church, too, with the majority of followers attending each and every week, making for a particularly friendly atmosphere. The priests themselves are extremely personable, as well. Instead, my reticence in not continuing to worship alongside Heidi is due to a sense of not belonging. Having too much respect for her and the other followers, the last thing I want is to act as a hypocrite by continuing to receive communion while being devoid of belief in a single supreme being.

Yet I cannot deny there is something else at work, some imposing force that is other worldly. After all, too many things seem to happen for a reason. From time to time I am enveloped by a deep sense that where I find myself on a daily basis is somehow preordained or meant to be. This seems true for the people in my life at a particular time or the job I find myself in or looking towards.

Rather than a central figure pulling the strings, I hold to a more amorphous view. From my humble standpoint it is the universe that is responsible, a cosmic energy source capable of the most advanced permutations. Thinking in these terms, I find it much easier to go along for the ride while freed of negativity, for God as a being and someone whose picture I can stare upon provides a source of anger when considering life's injustices and day to day frustrations. However, with the conceptualization of faith in a broad universe, I find it easier to accept the notion of a grander scheme.

Then again, who am I to say? My motto when it comes to matters of religion and spirituality is this: whatever helps you sleep at night. Never will I begrudge a person their faith in a God or Gods. Life is just too hard. Therefore, I feel that all means of making sense of the world through a higher power are truly special and worthy of the utmost respect. Besides, given my own struggles, I couldn't possibly pretend to have the only answer. Yet at least I now have one to work with, for which I am grateful.

CHAPTER FOURTEEN

Reality Testing

Heidi and I were officially wed on May 20th, 2001. We were married in Lake Ronkonkoma, New York, at Windows on the Lake. The afforded view does complete justice to the inn's name. The reception room, with its full length glass walls, leaves one staring out at a bright blue horizon. Held on a Sunday afternoon, the wedding ceremony took place under an outdoor gazebo.

It was a beautiful day on all fronts. The weather conditions were ideal. The temperature, as I recall, was in the mid-to-upper sixties, with blue skies and little wind to speak of. This helped make for optimal outdoor picture taking with family and friends. Of this we took full advantage.

There was also a very celebratory atmosphere. On my side of the family there seemed to be a deeper meaning to the whole event, as getting to that point must have been doubted along the way. In those touch and go moments of my recovery, it may have seemed unlikely to them that they would ever hear me utter the words "I do." As an added dimension, I won the heart of an able-bodied person, something in those early days my dad had envisioned. Though his vision was never revealed to me prior to becoming engaged, I had made my mind up long ago to never marry another person with a disability. It's not at all from being soured by my relationship with Maria. More than anything, staring at another wheelchair all day would be like looking in the mirror. It would end up being altogether too depressing, a constant reminder of my own disability. From a logistical standpoint, it also didn't make much sense. After all, who was going to reach the higher cabinets?

From the perspective of Heidi's family, I'd like to think their seemingly genuine display of happiness was for their daughter finding a worthy mate. To their credit, Heidi's parents had been good to me from the start. For this I will always be grateful, as they could have chosen to not be so accepting. There were *some* concerns, particularly of her mom, Barbara. Occasionally I'd get wind of her mother inquiring of Heidi how we were going to maintain an active sex life, given my physical limitations. This was apparently expressed as an important marital issue needing careful consideration before making a long term commitment to one person. While perhaps a bit personal in nature (and boy did it ever piss me off when made aware of this line of questioning), in the end I couldn't find a great deal of fault for such concerns. If the roles were reversed, I can't be so sure I'd act much differently. Given all the trouble that could have been caused by their daughter choosing to marry someone with a disability, I would say I got off pretty easy.

After the wedding we resumed our normal lives, both of us going back to work for one week before embarking on our honeymoon. For this grand event we chose a seven day cruise to the beautiful island of Bermuda. Without a care in the world, we had a fabulous time. We lived it up, taking in a vast majority of on-ship entertainment and participating in some of the most hilarious games and thematic contests. With seemingly a zip code of its own, there was always something to do on board. In fact, in what was previously considered a wholly foreign activity, together we became somewhat accomplished shuffleboard players. Then there was the food. Available day and night and seemingly without limit, it's amazing how the ship was able to make the return trip underneath the weight of its passengers.

At port there were a number of amazing sights to behold, in particular the beautiful landscape. With no on-land industry, there was an absence of pollution. The cities were by far the cleanest I had ever seen. The crystal blue waters were also to be marveled at. Owing as much as it does to tourism for its vitality, there was plenty of shopping to be done in Bermuda. I'd say we did more than our part to contribute to their bottom line. All in all, I couldn't have asked for a better time to have with my new bride. It was an entire week of marriage bliss that I won't ever forget.

I don't mean to imply this as the peak from which a descent began. Although it is true that, upon our return home, the fun and games were over. It was time for both of us to roll up our sleeves and get to work. After all, we had a marriage to get through.

That point hit home during the initial stages of living together. Not at all transient, these initial stages I speak of lasted for us a solid two years. It didn't help to be residing throughout that time in a one-bedroom apartment. Such close quarters do not allow for a lot of personal space. Severely limited options are available for getting away from each other in those times of greatest tension.

In the first place, though, we were both grateful to have found an accessible place to live. It's something we looked for a long time without much luck. Our assets did not dictate an ability to buy a house. Living at home was not an option, either. In fact, one of the most hurtful things said by my father at the time has since evolved into a family joke. He had threatened that if unable to find a place of our own, we'd be made to sleep in a tent in the backyard. In hindsight, I would like to think that if push came to shove, my childhood home would be extended to us on a temporary basis. The shame of it is that with my father it's very hard to tell. That's the part that hurt the most.

The main obstacle to finding an apartment lay in structural barriers. House apartments, with their inevitable inclusion of steps, were virtually out of the question and so we didn't bother much with intensive investigation on this front. However, even the seemingly latest architectural complexes did not meet our (okay, my) needs. This was surprising considering the already decade-old Americans with Disabilities Act (ADA) Laws. Doors were not wide enough or there were steps leading to entrance ways. After a few months of frustration it was cause for tremendous relief to have finally found something. Located in the town of Middle Island, our happy home was in a non-gated community of apartments.

But alas, our home was not always so happy. As we learned, being in love does not preclude a couple from some rather heated arguments. If anything, it seems a precursor of things to come. My, how the expletives would fly as we called each other out on our respective pet peeves, whether it was my constant nagging about turning off the light once exiting a room or Heidi's continued drone over my need to separate the laundry into a seemingly vast multitude of piles before washing.

Eventually you learn to pick your battles. For a marriage to work, it would seem impossible to nit pick about every little thing. Believe me, it saves a lot of negative energy and undue stress. So while it continues to be wholly important to bend to one another's expectations, it appears just as unrealistic that either person will achieve total conformity.

Along the same lines of how the *idea* of marriage differs from its actual experience, I cannot help but reflect on my career as a social worker. I consider myself no different from a vast majority of others who set their sights on work in the helping professions, in that I had a rather naïve frame of mind from the start. Setting myself up for a career path of working exclusively with individuals with disabilities, I had my mind set on making a distinctively positive mark on society. Believing with every fiber of my being that this was to be my true niche, I never entertained a thought of working with another population. It was going to be hospital social work or bust. Or so I had thought. As it turned out, the universe had another plan in mind.

Throughout grad school I was "stuck" with internships of which I originally wanted no part. My first year saw me work with the mentally ill in group homes. These were low-functioning clients who struggled in the accomplishment of basic activities of daily living, such as the preparation of simple meals and all aspects of proper hygiene. My responsibilities at the organization, Easter Seals of New Jersey, were mostly in the realm of observation and busy work. This was far from exciting stuff. Many of the group homes were not accessible, so that most of my time was spent back in the office. As such, there was little opportunity for clinical growth, a lack of ability to apply skills learned in the classroom. Unfortunately, some internship programs share this characteristic, with agency administrators putting little energy into the development of their future employees.

My enthusiasm for social work did not wane. That said, while at Easter Seals I witnessed firsthand the most jaded health care professional I've ever come across. In fact, she was downright nasty. With a perpetual scowl on her face, rarely, if ever, did she utter a nice word about her clients or coworkers. Such behavior was very difficult to grasp for this wide-eyed social worker to be. The display of negativity was all-encompassing and went beyond just having a bad day or two. Ultimately, I was left to wonder why this person would either choose to pursue or remain in a field she seemingly loathed. It couldn't be for the money, as no counselor I know of has ever seen a six-figure salary. Whatever the case, it does not seem possible to effectively serve people with needs if those same individuals are resented for *having* such needs. Here was my first introduction to social work not being a Pollyanna field, one that everybody comes to and stays with for all the right reasons.

Thankfully, my second internship was almost the complete opposite in its being a positive experience. Here I was surrounded by a sound leader and committed professionals ethically bound to serving their clients. However, once again I did not get to work with my desired population. Instead, I found myself among an altogether scary group of individuals, substance abusers. After all, drug addicts are among the lowest of the low. They are the dregs of society, a bunch of criminals who rape, kill, steal, and engage in all other types of nefarious acts. Ashamed to admit, these were the thoughts I carried to my first day of interning.

The substance abuse program to which I was assigned operated out of a hospital in Elizabeth, New Jersey. On an outpatient basis, from Monday through Friday, clients were in receipt of group and individual counseling for five hours per day, each session an hour in duration. Every day began with a meeting that included staff and clients alike. This was considered the first group of the day.

Such were the circumstances of my being introduced to about thirty or so addicts at once. Talk about culture shock. I was scared to death and on the verge of praying to make it out of there alive. Seriously, I was that uncomfortable. Hearing them talk about all the crimes they had committed and people they had emotionally scarred did not help matters. The final indignity came at the meeting's conclusion, when we were all to hold hands and form a circle. The Serenity Prayer was then recited in unison. For those unfamiliar, the verse is as follows: "God grant me the serenity to accept the things I can not change, the courage to change the things I can, and the wisdom to know the difference." Great, I thought, now religion was involved. I vowed never to return.

Return I did, though, and I was glad for it. For without going back, the opportunity to learn a valuable lesson would have been missed. With each passing day I came to appreciate having more in common with those clients than I ever would have imagined. There is a shared experience of loss. The individual in recovery must grieve the inability to engage in drug-using behaviors. Having worked in the field for over seven years, I've come to realize this is not a trite statement. For the true addict, there is no such thing as just stopping. Believe me, I used to think it was that easy. That was before I was introduced to the disease concept. According to this now widely-held principle, there is a physiological aspect to addiction whereby the human brain becomes chemically altered through the continued use of drugs and alcohol.

As part of a natural process, the brain produces chemicals called neurotransmitters that help to determine our mood. When stimulated, as in the case of a runner's high, we feel happy and energized. Conversely, the depletion of these chemicals, such as endorphins and serotonin, can leave us feeling depressed and sluggish. Located in the pleasure center of the brain, the neurotransmitters become crazed with activity once drugs enter our system. The consequence of long term use is that the body gets lazy, figuring it should not have to work so hard when it's being regularly stimulated by a foreign substance. The outcome is addiction, the body unmercifully craving what was once produced in abundance on its own.

Once addiction sets in, tremendous work must be done to remain clean and sober. For over ninety percent of chemically dependent people, this entails attending self help groups such as Alcoholics Anonymous and Narcotics Anonymous. A healthy support system is deemed critical to keeping the addiction in check. And as with any disease, recovery is seen as a lifelong process. There is no known cure to speak of. That is why healthcare professionals use the qualifier of "remission" when affixing a diagnosis on an addict with several years of sobriety.

Ultimately, I was forced to consider that I did not have to work exclusively with people who had disabilities in order to positively influence the population being served. Instead of getting caught up in the specifics of the situation, it was important for me to realize that feelings, those instrumental building blocks of behavioral change, are universal and as such span myriad ailments. I can not reiterate often enough how I've found that such acceptance is the key to a healthy and productive lifestyle. My own experience dictates that resentment is the byproduct of a lack of acceptance.

Yet as graduate school approached its conclusion, I once again made a pitch toward working with people with disabilities. I would end up sending a resume to the human resources department of every hospital on Long Island. My search was not too restricted, however, as I sought employment at all places possible for my degree.

Wouldn't you know that all my callbacks ended up being from substance abuse treatment agencies. It seemed that my original concern was warranted, that the population served on my internships had pigeonholed me to this one concentration of social work. That being said, the old adage of "beggars can't be choosers" came into play. This was especially true considering the school loan totals staring me in the face. So it was that my first two full-time jobs in my chosen profession were in the setting of outpatient drug and alcohol rehabilitation.

In each instance I gained more experience than could ever be learned from a book. Sure, my progression through higher education was necessary when it came to job performance. Without it, I would have been completely lost. However, the knowledge of the thing took on a whole new light in its application. As one example, it was extremely eye-opening to be exposed to so much paperwork. I got into the field to help people, not to push paper seemingly three quarters of the day. Yet that was indeed the reality. There were treatment plans, progress notes, monthly reports to referral sources such as parole and probation, and much too lengthy psychosocial assessments. Deadlines abounded, to the point that administration seemed to harp more on the timely completion of documentation than deciphering the quality of interventions provided to each client.

Taken by surprise, I was quite overwhelmed early in my career. It was not uncommon to find myself lying awake at night fretting about job loss. Thanks to some hard work I was able to persevere. I decided from the start to adopt a "whatever-it-takes" attitude. At times this meant showing up for work early, staying late, or even doing what I could from home. Eventually, I was able to accept the fact that excessive paperwork was simply part of the job. As much as I loathed it, there was no way to fight against it. Resistance was futile. Now, that doesn't mean an absence of frustration, especially as new forms were developed from above and added to the daily routine. It wasn't like we clinicians had anything else to do!

The other instance of on-the-job training came in the form of navigating coworker relationships. From the start, I completely looked forward to working as part of a collaborative team. To be sure, such camaraderie is one of the most important aspects of any occupation. In social work the import lies in the emotionally stressful nature of the position, something preeminent in the provision of services to substance abusers.

What makes this population so special is the tremendously high rate of relapse and recidivism. Accordingly, the measure of one's success as a clinician must be reevaluated. It's very much a "pie in the sky" mentality to expect total abstinence from day one in an outpatient program. This is especially true for those including, but not limited to, long term addicts who may find themselves in treatment for the first time, those with chronic relapse, repetitive legal offenders, and youths who think they're invincible.

No matter what the case may be, I do not mean to convey that the use of substances by a client was ever condoned. However, I witnessed time and again how relapse could be processed as a learning experience. Chances are people, places, and things got in the way of long term sobriety. Just as with any other example of learning from one's mistakes, by internalizing the precursors of relapse, an addict can significantly strengthen his or her recovery. That, my friends, is a measure of true success.

Then there were the clients totally resistant to the treatment process. Of this type there were plenty, perhaps as many as nine out of ten. Prone to viewing counselors as their enemies and blaming everyone but themselves for how life had turned to shit, they were loathe to take suggestions and usually dropped out during the early stages of treatment. Mandated by the courts to complete a drug and alcohol program, not complying meant there was a significant risk of incarceration. Surely in a situation such as this there can be no inkling of personal success. Not so fast, though. The hope in these cases is that you at least touched clients in a way that, in looking back, something you said provided a trigger toward positive self improvement. In the world of the substance abuse counselor this is the only way to get some sleep at night. Some people just aren't ready to change even though you are more than willing to help. As a golden rule, in order for change to occur, a clinician cannot work harder than their client.

Truly unfortunate in all this is the fact that staff can be just as sick as the people they are hoping to treat. This played itself out at my second full-time place of employment, which lasted from October 2002 to November 2006. Starting out as a regular line worker, it was originally a great place to work. There existed a friendly atmosphere conducive to a high degree of productivity. My first day was spent at training, where I was made to feel welcome to the organization. Consisting of a number of different satellite offices outside the corporate headquarters, every year the entire umbrella of employees were treated to a day-long holiday party on company time. This helped establish a sense of community. Also, with a number of interagency workshops offered, there appeared to be a strong commitment to employee growth and development.

All that would change as I progressed through the ranks and the company began to expand. In the summer of 2003 I became coordinator of the evening outpatient program. It was a position that opened up rather suddenly due to the firing of my direct supervisor. A coworker and I were the whistleblowers about his soliciting fireworks from one of my clients. Such behavior is amongst the top items on the ethical "not to do" list and ended up costing him his job. Soliciting any type of favor from a client creates a relationship of power that cannot be tolerated. Basically, it comes down to the fact that it's never okay to take advantage of a client's vulnerability.

From my new "seat" I was subjected to an entirely new experience, being supervised by the director of the agency, a moderately attractive middle-aged woman named Dee. A social worker with vast clinical experience, very early on we discovered a connection between us. It turned out that her children and I were around the same age and attended high school together, though I could not recall knowing either of them. Furthermore, she had lived just a block away from my childhood home and was struck by the fact that I was the same person she remembered hearing about being involved in a major car accident.

With this history you'd think Dee and I would be relatively close in regards to our working relationship. Yet while our relationship was cordial at first, in my new position it did not remain that way for long. And why would it, anyway? After all, I had witnessed Dee at her worst with others. Talk about someone who didn't practice what they preached, Dee claimed unceasingly to not be a fan of the alcoholic family. The main characteristic of such is that members have to tiptoe around the household figurehead for fear of disturbing the peace. For all her protestations, of this Dee was the main culprit. At any given point in time, at least one staff member was in the barrel of her ever-watchful eye.

She'd make it known to you, also, as to who she was targeting. Countless times behind the closed doors of supervisory meetings, I would be treated to her rants against whomever was out of favor at the time. There was no holding back, either. As if berating a person's work performance wasn't enough, it was not uncommon for Dee to call into question a fellow coworker's sexual orientation or some other private aspect of their lives that was absolutely none of her business.

Another tactic was to not talk to the "out" person at all. She played the part of the "bad mommy" for all it was worth. Here she was, the supposed leader of our branch of the larger organization, at times not even acknowledging the existence of her own staff. Simply deplorable stuff, if you ask me. Adding another layer to the sickness, this could all change at a moment's notice when someone else screwed up. That's exactly why it did no good to suck up to her, as many tried. Engaging in such brown nosing behavior only contributed toward feeling worse when *your* time came. In the long run, being overly nice was not paid back in kind.

Eventually I was subjected to much the same, and needless to say it was not a good feeling. The turning point came when I didn't get as emotionally invested as she did in what was to be my first state-sponsored audit as program coordinator. Here the rules changed dramatically in mid-stream. As the operating license of the agency neared its expiration, I had spoken with Dee for months prior about being quite anxious to pass the impending state audit with flying colors. As with all things, I wanted badly to succeed.

All along, the response to my nervousness was, "take it easy." I was assured from the top that perfection was not expected given the large volume of clients and limited staffing conditions endured by the evening program. Granted, I was still a bit stressed in making sure that a select list of most important items to monitor in client charts was cared for effectively. That said, my supervisor's direction served to put my mind at significant ease. Boy, was that ever short-lived, as when the state did arrive, Dee just about lost her mind.

She put the entire agency on virtual lockdown. Time-off requests were ruled null and void. It was all hands on deck, truly unfortunate for me since of all days the Office of Alcohol & Substance Abuse Services (OASAS) decided to rear their ugly heads on June 28! Dee's expectations changed dramatically as every chart suddenly had to be inspected with a fine-toothed comb. Even under the best of circumstances this was an overwhelming project. However, given just twenty-four hour's notice before the state intended to inspect our records made for a seemingly impossible task.

On top of being emotionally drained on my most horrible day of the year, I was also physically spent as I did not leave the office until just before midnight. Granted, the extra hours of preparation definitely paid off. Our operating license was restored without a single blemish, something entirely unheard of. The only problem was that the successful outcome was deemed to be no thanks to me. I was taken totally aback by this turn of events as I was presented with the news of being placed on probation for what amounted to not working as a team player.

This was a tough pill to swallow. I had an extremely difficult time functioning in the weeks and months ahead. I had a lot of trouble sleeping and my appetite was nonexistent. Experiencing a tenuous employment status for the very first time, my thoughts even turned to suicide. Home alone one night, I took inventory of the medicine cabinet, settling on a tall bottle of Tylenol PM. Conducting due diligence with online research, I discovered this to be an unreliable method. And while a steak knife to the gut would surely do the job, I just couldn't bear the idea of Heidi having such a severe mess to clean up.

By far, the hardest thing was to figure out exactly what I did that was so egregious. Asking this of Dee revealed that throughout the audit process I had spoken nastily toward other staff. I could not recall behaving in any such way, and despite many inquiries the exact nature of my supposed statements was never made clear.

From a more analytical viewpoint, I was able to move past being overly depressed and angry. Through a continued discourse that included mainly my wife and grandparents, I was able to reconcile that it wasn't me. Instead, I was able to more correctly consider Dee's pattern of past behavior. It was a good thing, too, because my work environment was on a precipitous decline. Dee made herself conspicuously unavailable for providing any kind of consistent supervision. Furthermore, she seemed to search long and hard on a daily basis for any blemish she could pin on me. The scrutiny was severe enough that I fantasized about quitting at every free moment.

Some three months later, I finally got my wish. However, it wasn't before a number of failed interviews. With my sole focus on escaping a bad situation, I no doubt came across to potential employers as desperate. It all came together, though, as I consciously began to relax and heeded my wife's advice to develop greater patience. Doing so allowed me to thoroughly enjoy our pre-planned vacation to Disney World in celebration of Heidi's thirtieth birthday.

Just a few days prior to our departure, I went on my best interview yet. I got the job, and it turned out to be just the break I needed, in more ways than one. I didn't end up leaving for just anywhere; instead I found myself serving a more personally self-fulfilling population in the elderly and people with disabilities. Hired as a case manager for Health Partners of New York (HPNY), I work for a managed long term care program. It's a mouthful, I know. Having since been taken over by GuildNet, we're an insurance company that secures services for people meeting certain criteria, helping them remain in the community instead of residing in nursing homes.

In addition to the feeling of making a greater difference in people's lives, I'm also making more money with increased vacation time and better health benefits. All this and I actually have fewer job responsibilities! No longer am I in charge of an entire program. Gone are the headaches associated with report writing, statistics gathering, and staff management.

I must admit to having suffered a blow to the ego simultaneous with returning to a regular line-worker position. By being "the man," there existed an added air of personal importance. Mentally I had been able to stroke myself for this accomplishment. Coping with such an adjustment was made easier through the self reminder of not having anything to prove by ascending toward the zenith of any organization. Power does not necessarily bring with it happiness. This I have experienced firsthand.

I am much happier now, that's for sure. The ability to focus exclusively on my own work is completely refreshing. After all, perhaps the greatest frustration I experienced as a manager was the powerlessness of delegating tasks that were ultimately not performed to my personal standards. Another satisfactory aspect of HPNY/GuildNet is the lack of dysfunctional relationships between coworkers and superiors. Caught up as I was in the world of my previous employer, being exposed to a more genuine atmosphere has been eye opening and a welcome change.

Still, what I went through with my previous employer had a hardening effect. Especially in the case of superiors, I am more on the lookout for dysfunctional behavior than ever before. That is not a bad thing, either. At least now I may be better equipped to see it coming.

By no means do I wish to imply that my current job is perfect in every way. After all, it would seem there's a bad side to every job. Of the few annoyances I do encounter on a daily basis, one is that I am on the phone all day. I hate the phone. I'd much rather talk in person and do not enjoy being unable to see whose on the other end of the line. Coinciding with this irritation is the fact that I now have no client contact. Accustomed to a career of performing individual and group therapy, this has made for quite an adjustment. It is something I miss and may wish to supplement with a part-time counseling position at a hospital or treatment agency. Then again, who needs the extra work? Finally, perhaps the most disconcerting aspect of my job is the fact that we work in cubicles, so that almost nothing said on the phone is sacred. That's alright, though, as these issues have all but smoothed over with increased familiarity.

Pretty much universal for all social work positions, I cannot forget to mention as a drawback the relative shortcoming of financial reimbursement. Put quite frankly, no one should expect to make a killing in this profession. Of course there are exceptions to every rule, especially for those inclined to devote more than a fair share of time and patience toward the development of a successful private practice. While I have certainly flirted with the idea (even going so far as to print my own business cards), nothing has come to fruition. In fact, I've stopped trying altogether. Simply put, I just don't have the passion for it right now. Never say never though, I suppose.

So while the bills get paid, a rich man I am not. My wife and I adhere to a strict budget and save for a major vacation taken once per year. A little money hungry, I sometimes lament not foreseeing the accomplishment of a childhood dream – becoming a millionaire by the age of forty. Still, I can't imagine doing anything else.

CHAPTER FIFTEEN

The Elephant

In the setting of treatment, as in life, there is a phenomenon known as the "elephant in the living room." It is a wholly figurative beast that represents a weighty issue or issues recognized by all members of a particular social system yet addressed by no one. It represents family secrets that breed denial.

By no means have I ever been above my clients in this way. In fact, there is often a precariously thin line separating a legally mandated client from their counselor. The difference mainly comes down to decision making, counselors practicing thoughtful meditation on all possible consequences and choosing the path of least destruction.

There have existed a number of "elephants" in the history of my own family system, one pertaining to the relationship between me and my father. As evidenced by a writer's block I've been experiencing lately, there has been considerable uncertainty regarding the best way to proceed with its description. What seems most appropriate is starting with a personal journal entry, dated November 14th 2000, penned late at night. Without further editing, it says:

> I just now had the most amazing conversation
> with my father as I've had my entire life. In
> all I have finally figured out, thanks to his help,
> why I have resented him so much for almost
> my whole life. It all goes back to my accident,
> as so many things in my life do. I haven't
> evolved past the dynamics of our relationship as
> it was back then, with Dad always pushing me
> as I needed to be then and me not being
> allowed to disagree with him because the stakes
> were so damn high. I mean life or death. You
> hear the cliché 'life or death situation.' Well

I was there. On the one side was my Mom, more the nurturer than he throughout that whole ordeal. I've always found it easier to approach my mother and talk with her as a peer. Not with Dad though. He's always been in my head that person you could not disagree with or have a different opinion than and have it be ok. I've always in my own head had to have his approval or think if he does not approve a decision I make than he disapproves of me. But after tonight I see him as just a man, not the authority figure status that hasn't changed since I've been nine years old. This is such a different time now. He expressed not even wanting that role any longer. It's all me! Its funny how my relationship with my father is the only difficult one in my life. Funny because the answer was so obvious I couldn't even see it. Or perhaps I chose not to see it. I mean how could I have missed it all these years unless I didn't want it to be found. This is an issue between the two of us for so many years, visited over and over again without any improvement. I really feel like a breakthrough has occurred tonight. I just feel different, so much insight has been gained.

There you have it. Don't get me wrong though, the resentment I speak of hardly ever played itself out in living color. There was an absence altogether of overt maliciousness, at least from my perspective. Rather it mostly lay just below the surface, manifesting itself through standoffishness and otherwise disengaging behaviors. Not having learned, after my recovery, to just relax around my father had far reaching consequences. For instance, I do not recall ever debating the merits of an opinion he had to offer, whatever the subject matter. This held true even when I personally disagreed or could provide facts to the contrary of what was being espoused. Exactly what I was afraid of if I didn't hold back was completely beyond me. Never having raised a hand to me, it would seem beyond irrational to foresee any subsequent abuse given his expressions of thankfulness for my just being alive.

Perhaps the saddest consequence of the disconnect between me and my father was the lost opportunity to develop a real friendship. Jealousy strikes when I hear of others experiencing such enjoyment. Like a snowball rolling downhill, there was an unfortunate momentum that carried such possibility farther away. For that I will mostly take the hit, as on many occasions I turned down the opportunity to speak with a licensed therapist. My own stubbornness in not taking my parents up on this offer proved costly. Looking back, some of the emotional issues faced after my trauma may have been far less exacerbating had I been engaged in professional help from a young age. Then again, perhaps the choice shouldn't have been left for me to make in the first place. Indeed, I always feel it heartwarming when parents in recovery see to it that their young children receive counseling services. So many dynamics change in the aftermath of traumatic events. No child should be expected to handle such weighty issues on their own.

The shame of it is that at times I really could have used a friend in which to confide. The possibility of a friendship appeared while relaxing on our front porch after my first year of college. My father asked point blank whether I had tried smoking marijuana. By that time I had. While growing up, smoking anything of any kind had been deemed completely off limits. The phrase of warning if ever caught doing so was, "I brought you into this world and I can take you out of it." A daunting prospect if ever there was one. With these words ringing in my head, I did my best to shrug off my father's question. It didn't project with any conviction, and so, I'd been caught. What happened next came as a complete surprise. He didn't freak out, but only questioned my obvious fear of being severely berated. In the end, he respected that I was grown and was going to experiment in new environments.

Another example took place when I purchased my first vehicle, a 1996 Chevy full-sized van, and first began to drive. I actually bought the car in the summer of 1997. It was brand new and sitting on the lot as a leftover; I ended up getting a pretty good deal on it. Of course, some modifications had to occur and I wasn't able to take full advantage of my new purchase for a few months. Obtaining my license some two years prior through a local adaptive driver education program, it had been that long since I was behind the wheel.

The van's readiness for my use coincided with the halfway point of my first semester at Rutgers University. My father proposed that I make the nothing short of gut-wrenching drive back to school from our home in Long Island. To this day, it's a story we reminisce about as one of the most daring feats of all time. A mere novice behind the wheel, I could have seriously maimed, if not killed us outright. And even though we arrived safe and none the worse for wear, I was happy beyond belief upon the trip's conclusion.

Having Dad in the passenger seat was then and for years thereafter among the most nerve-wracking of experiences. Regressing back to the roles of more than a decade prior, I put a tremendous amount of pressure on myself to succeed in his presence. As often happened in these cases, my efforts backfired to the point of losing sight of all the fine details that must be attended to in order to be a safe driver. Errors that would have been avoided if I'd just relaxed a little included not yielding properly, parking outside of line designations, and even misjudging a stop light or two.

Especially as it related to my father, I had a difficult time seeing my parents as regular people, themselves fallible and not beyond reproach. This hit home in particular when I came into possession of a newspaper article written in the local rag in the early 1970's. Inset was a picture of my dad riding the waves on a surfboard, a favorite pastime of his as a teenager and throughout early adulthood. He appeared so very young and strong looking. It helped me to see him in this time, before I was born, with his whole future on the horizon. Doing so confirmed how we are all in the process of finding our way, with perfection foreign to all things human.

I now share a satisfying relationship with my father. It's extremely liberating not having to hide my personal thoughts and feelings due to concerns about his disapproval. Although there may be disagreement, it does not mean that he is "right" and I am "wrong" to act in a certain way. All it means is that we disagree. I'm okay with that today. At long last my mindset has shifted toward perceiving my father as a peer rather than a person of supreme authority.

Back to "elephants" again, another metaphorical one took the shape of my mother's experience of guilt for allowing me to proceed on that doomed bicycle ride. Her concern regarded the length of the trip she allowed me to take, in hindsight thinking it an inappropriate course for her nine year old son to handle. She revealed as much when I was in the greatest depths of my own depression. It was 1994, that crossing of the line to more years spent in the chair than not.

Mind you, I had always suspected that my mom held herself accountable for my injury. From a common sense perspective, how could she not? After all, it was her decision alone that sent me on my way. What had not in prior times been revealed, though, was the main source of her self-blame. Once expressed, I was able to remind her in letter form of that first bicycle trip of some thirteen miles, taken with my neighborhood pals and their father, which she had completely forgotten to take into account. I went on to convey that in no way had I ever considered her at fault for what happened to me. To this day, Mom is fond of sharing how she still reads my now fifteen year old document on occasion. I'm glad beyond words to have been able to ease some of my mother's pain. No one person except the man who hit me should take the brunt of responsibility for my injury.

Finally, there was for me an internal "elephant" fostered through many years of denial. For a very long time I had it in mind to leave New York State. Such longing was forever under the guise of wanting to live in a warmer climate. As any person in a wheelchair will tell you, the winter months can be altogether too cruel when it comes to personal mobility. Snow and ice are almost impossible to traverse independently. Not to mention the cold itself. My body having lost the ability to efficiently regulate when it comes to severe ranges in temperature, once a chill seeps in it is hard to get rid of. Given this reality, it would seem to make sense that I'd belong in a place like Florida, Arizona, or Southern California. Then there's my seasonal attitude. From November through March I could be incredibly short with people and at times difficult to deal with due to an underlying experience of depression.

Now, if I were to be completely honest with myself, I don't fare much better in the heat. While summer is a season to which I generally look forward, my issue of being unable to sweat precludes an ability to remain outside for extended periods. My body can handle about an hour of exposure to ninety degree temperatures. Beyond that I risk losing all energy for the rest of the day. Still, there's no doubt that my overall outlook improves during summer. It turns out this has everything to do with an increased exposure to light. Making this connection in graduate school led to being diagnosed with Seasonal Affective Disorder (SAD), a mental illness recognized by the Diagnostic and Statistical Manual of Mental Disorders. (In its fourth major revision, this is the bible of social workers, an in-depth listing of all ailments of the mind.) For the past eight years I have been taking the antidepressant Zoloft during daylight savings time when we lose an hour of daylight. Since that time my overall mood has been much more stable on a year-round basis. Honestly speaking as well, especially during winter months I do not entirely mind being stuck in the house. For one, there's something to be said for being all wrapped up in a cozy blanket while reading or watching television. Also, when it comes down to it, I am quite the homebody. On most weekends I'm perfectly content not to venture out for any reason.

So my desire to move really had nothing to do with the weather. Its sole purpose was to escape the vicinity where my accident took place. It's the same phenomenon I encountered many times as a substance abuse counselor. Addicts in early recovery would regularly express the belief that all their problems would disappear if they could just "get out of Dodge." Here the success rate is exceedingly slim, as drugs can be found anywhere if they are looked for hard enough. As with me, people bring themselves along to whatever environment they inhabit. Problems are taken along for the ride, the classic case of "wherever you go there you are." So the key for the addict or otherwise is not to become a slave to maladaptive behavior patterns. This I have avoided by becoming more at peace with the circumstances surrounding my accident. Gone now is an unrelenting desire to leave the state I have always loved, for its rich history and place within the consciousness of the world.

One thing for which I give my parents a ton of credit is not letting my accident itself become an "elephant." Thankfully, there was always an open line of communication around this subject. My own personal hotline was available to be accessed 24 hours a day, 7 days a week. While at times severely underutilized, the fact that it was available provided comfort enough so that I was not left to experience any shame surrounding the trauma. Furthermore, I'll be forever grateful to my mother and father for never blaming me in any way for the accident. When spoken about, it was always in the context of being a terrible occurrence that we were all working very hard to overcome. I recognize now that any other approach would have had a dramatically negative impact on my psyche, certainly wreaking havoc on my self esteem and ability to function optimally in society.

Unfortunately, I've witnessed such ignorance play itself out in a few instances in which the mere acknowledgement of someone's disability within the family system is deemed entirely off limits. Doing this accomplishes nothing but stunting family growth toward a point where there can be some humorous banter about the disability without someone becoming extremely uptight. In my opinion, an opportunity is needed to have some laughs at the expense of the disability. Full acknowledgement is an important beginning step in this process.

CHAPTER SIXTEEN

Only the Beginning

"Success" is a term loaded with subjectivity. It makes for a great interview subject, one used by my former supervisor when she asked applicants how they would judge their own success after a year's worth of work. In similar fashion, I think the question bears contemplation on how successful one's life has been up to its end. For me there is no question what I want for my epitaph. I simply want it noted that I did the best with what I had. To me there is no greater compliment. That I didn't short-change myself of the only opportunity for a full life experience despite certain challenges ranks as my highest success.

In tune with this, I consider it a great success to have avoided being a burden to my parents. While they would vehemently contest this choice of words, by "burden" I mean to say that my hard-won independence has allowed them to resume their own lives. I do not require their constant care and attention, something that can't be said for others with a disabled child. Heck, dependence even goes beyond families affected by disability. With pride, I became among the first of my neighborhood peers to leave the nest. Me, with seemingly the most strikes against being able to do so.

I derive substantial pleasure from considering my parents ability to enjoy their golden years to the absolute fullest. Come to think of it, there's a certain degree of amazement that they're still together. As you'd imagine, my accident took a significant toll on their relationship. At times there were constant arguments. They separated twice, briefly when I was in tenth grade and for a lengthier period in 1993-94. The first separation was harder on me than the second. Aside from me being older, communication between my parents had deteriorated so much that the idea of them being apart was a relief. Needless to say, they reconciled and have been able to make their marriage work ever since.

Generally speaking, the way life has turned out, there's little choice but to laugh away the years of worry that I'd ever get to this point. In the past, too much focus was directed toward different problems, feeding into a long-standing state of depression obvious to most despite my best efforts to keep it hidden. Now in times of stress and doubt I conjure up the image of an old single-cell Ziggy comic strip. At the bottom of a huge staircase stands the main character, a rather short and pudgy middle-aged man of no great distinction. The caption reads something like this: "Do not measure yourself by the obstacles you face. Instead measure yourself by those you've already faced up to."

Indeed, why *not* start to look at things in a more positive light? It may feel as uncomfortable as a brand new wardrobe but there's really nothing to lose. In my previous work with addicts, a central goal was for clients to understand how negative consequences are born from negative attitudes and behaviors. During their time spent in treatment, encouragement is provided to adopt a recovery-oriented lifestyle. If given a fair chance but not met with positive results, there's always the choice of reverting back to the prior way of doing things. I don't know of one person who could honestly say that their lives were better in the year prior to successful completion of the outpatient program.

I would like to impart some other thoughts to you, my reader. Never prone to lecturing or sitting on a high horse, if I could express only one piece of advice based on my own experience, it would be to avoid obsessive worry. Don't get me wrong, I consider a healthy concern for life circumstances quite necessary. After all, without some degree of caution the decision-making process would be too haphazard, with insufficient energy devoted to consequential thinking. On the other hand, when carried to excess, we fail to recognize the goodness of the moment. Each moment wasted in this way can't be relived due to not being valued in the first place.

Worthy as it may be, this business of remaining fully present at all times is difficult to achieve. One of the true mentors in my career uses the 'Where's Waldo?' cartoon as a metaphor for staying in the moment. In this scenario, Waldo represents you. Just as in the cartoon, where the objective is to locate Waldo in a picture filled with distractions, so the individual is challenged to find and center themselves amidst the chaos that so often constitutes everyday life.

Speaking of life, that old cliché holds true about it being too short, the years flying by with increased velocity. Yet at any given age, we may think we have all the time in the world. As this is oftentimes not the case, I fear there are too many people who, at the end stage of their lives, strive in desperation to continue. Of course, by then it's entirely too late to realize there's seldom a perfect time for anything.

On the other hand, it makes sense that people who have lived the fullest lives may be least fearful of dying. I seek to be part of this group. In respect to finances, while fiscal responsibility is a worthy characteristic, I allowed myself for years to be shackled with over-thinking the "what ifs." However, the truth of the matter is that you can't plan for everything. And while a vacation to Disney World may curtail the ability to contribute more money toward savings, such trips are what enhance the experience of life. While I don't possess many fears, a major source of terror is looking back on a life unlived.

For my money, "as good as it gets" in life is to be at peace with oneself. Being centered in this way was a quality I always envied in others. It seemed so elusive because for several years I wanted to be anybody *but* myself, so much so that I was willing to pay a very hefty price. As an illustration, after completing my rehabilitation at RUSK I was sent a brief questionnaire. Among their inquiries was whether I'd consider undergoing a hypothetical procedure which had the potential to increase my level of functioning but whose risk was such that my condition could also become worse. Without any hesitation I responded with a resounding "yes."

I meet the same question today with the completely opposite answer. While experiencing even the slightest increase in functioning would of course be welcome, there's no way I would now sign off on the risk of losing any of the muscle control I currently hold dear. To this extent, I have achieved the euphoria of inner peace.

In closing, I must admit that having to do it all over again, this is not the life I would have chosen. Given the circumstances, I'd challenge anyone in my position to think differently. With the paralysis, elimination issues, and accessibility concerns, my life at times is far from fun. I won't lie and say I haven't spent at least some time and energy considering the sacrifices I'd make if the chance were presented to be counted among the completely able-bodied.

Making this sort of deal with the devil is the stuff of story. In reality, the question becomes, "What am I going to do with this feeling?" To deny its presence will most assuredly guarantee continued negativity. Still, there can be no doubt that life is just plain easier if not spent in a wheelchair. If nothing else, it eliminates having to deal with a mountain of ignorance.

Then again, if my accident had not occurred, would I even be alive today? Did what almost killed me actually end up saving my life? Agonizing over such unknowns has never ceased to be a source of personal torment. As a solution, I have found it much more helpful to entrust such matters to the universe. Perhaps there is a plan in place that will forever remain beyond my immediate comprehension. Control, to the extent of not being a complete illusion, is limited to that which lies directly ahead. So today I vow to do all that *can* be done, and that is to keep on pushing.

CONCLUSION

I would like to take this opportunity to share observations about my writing process. Put simply, it was long and arduous. The formal writing of this work began in late February of 2005. Encouraged by my wife, we drove to Walmart one evening and I purchased a standard three-subject notebook. With that, I took her suggestion and started writing stories in my new ledger. So it came to pass that on a nightly basis I'd write a one to two page account of some significant event from my past. It turned out to be a particularly important method, one that helped alleviate feeling overwhelmed by the prospect of producing hundreds of pages of material. Also, I didn't concern myself with keeping the events in any particular order. Whatever came to mind, I wrote.

I proceeded this way for about a month before gaining some idea on how the book would be started. Only then did the transfer to word processor begin to take place. Feeling quite giddy about the show of progress, it occurred to me that the work might be completed by summer's end. Despite the doubt expressed by my better half, while perhaps a bit ambitious, I did not consider being far off in my prediction. Having finished more than three years later, boy was I ever wrong.

What I hadn't considered was the emotional strain provoked by the writing process. My mind's eye was brought to places unvisited for quite some time, leading to the occasional hiatus in writing. Most difficult were the flood of memories from early childhood, consistently producing a dull ache deep within. I can't imagine this feeling will ever completely go away, nor do I think it necessarily should. Though entirely too brief, my life before being injured is part of my legacy.

Another emotional stumbling block was coming to terms with actions I wish I could retract that are completely separate from the circumstances of my accident. To live an examined life is not the easiest means of existence. In fact, this taking of a moral inventory can be most difficult. If done with honesty, coming face to face with personal short-comings is emotionally uncomfortable. The desire for escape can be powerful, as warts appear so much uglier when not covered.

But with vulnerability comes also the freedom of putting oneself out there for all to see. This is my life, and for the first time I am prepared to claim it as such without shame. The same holds true for occurrences both within and beyond my immediate control. Taken in the right context, there are no mistakes, only learning experiences upon which to build. Why not repeat those behaviors that met with the greatest success, while making sure those yielding negative results are modified or done away with altogether? Now if only I and the rest of humanity could commit to this practice on a daily basis, what a wonderful world this would be.

There remained two additional reasons for not finishing this book in a timelier manner. A night owl at heart, my initial routine consisted of writing into the small hours of the morning, hitting my stride between midnight and 2 a. m. Working evenings at the time made for a perfect arrangement. However, that would change with my hiring at HPNY. Now working a shift of 8:30 a. m. – 4:30 p. m., I cannot stay up so late. I also require a minimum of eight hours of sleep in order to function properly. All things considered, getting used to my new schedule was harder than anticipated. Though left without much choice, even now I find daytime writing extremely forced.

Finally, about mid-way through the memoir, I became filled with doubt that coincided with losing sight of the original goal. Regrettably, my focus shifted toward publication and money making, rather than writing for the more profound good of painting a word picture because I considered it meaningful. I became consumed with worry about how my book would be received by literary critics. Seen through this different pair of eyes, it became too overwhelming to think any type of mass production was possible. Also, it seemed the publication process had too many obstacles to overcome. I was gripped by paralysis of another sort, the "what's the point" kind that held me from continuing.

I persevered by drawing on one of the most important lessons from my father. Namely, I reminded myself of his endless encouragement to place greater emphasis on the process rather than the result of an undertaking. According to this way of thinking, if adequate effort is put into a project, the outcome will take care of itself. Whether applied toward writing, fitness, or test taking, I have found this to be true time and again.

Despite the above challenges, I consider the writing of this book to have been a profoundly enjoyable experience. Having a forum for the open expression of my inner thoughts and feelings was extremely cathartic. That so much was retrieved from the vast reaches of my memory was a pleasant surprise. The initial concern of not having enough material was thankfully alleviated. With each new idea were born two or three others that required documenting.

One aspect I tried to steer clear of was coming across as preachy. Something that disturbs me about books on self-improvement is their professorial nature, the idea that following a few simple rules will result in eternal bliss. While offering some of my own opinions, I recognize myself as a flawed human being who gets caught up in the muck of life and becomes distracted from practicing what I opine are worthy attitudes and behaviors. I do not shy away from my status as an internally fractured individual needing continuous inner work to maintain a modicum of peace and genuine happiness.

By far the most satisfying outcome of writing this book is fulfilling a goal I set out to accomplish years ago. To me there are few better feelings than the peace of mind that accompanies goal attainment. And though the prospect of death still does not bestow a great deal of comfort, I will now be able to rest easier having produced a detailed account of my existence.

APPENDIX

My Poetry

TOUCHING SUMMER

Green grass, green trees
For as far as the eye can see
The sun beats down upon my face
I wish to be no other place

Birds chirp, children play
Laughter escapes and lasts all day
I sit outside reading my book
While butterfly colors deserve a good look

Lemonade stands, crowded beaches
Drive in movies play double features
Boys and girls wading in pools
Me in shorts and staying cool

Garage sales, vacation drives
Bees buzzing in their hives
How I long for this time of year
The warming breeze saying summer's here

OVERCOMING NIGHTMARES

Hospital memories come floating in
Where do they come from I wonder aloud
A life so hard, where to begin
Like looking for sky in a trampling crowd

Miserable images of suffering and pain
Flood my dreams in the blackened night
Why must I live this over again?
When all I'm left is panic and fright

There I am at 9 with a trache
Lying helpless, tubes in my chest
Needles in places I no longer ache
Right leg in traction, many nights of unrest

A nurse's bell that fails to work
Labored breathing like a drowning man
Uncontrolled bowels, lying in mirk
Not able to move in this quicksand

Yet, another take is perhaps in order
Thankfulness may be the key to this mystery
Instead of viewing myself as less than a quarter
To see such progress from an unfortunate history

Fast forwarding to the present brings relief
Holding a job, being married and stable
With no obligation to live in grief
Delighting in that which I bring to the table

NEVER GIVE UP

Do what you will, I'll never give up
While life is a drill, I'll never give up
When you think I've had enough, I'll never give up
For although life is tough, I'll never give up
I'll never give up

Smack me again, I'll never give up
Leave me for dead, I'll never give up
If my luck is all bad, I'll never give up
You'll just make me madder, I'll never give up
I'll never give up

Bring on the stress, I'll never give up
You may expect less, I'll never give up
No matter the lump, I'll never give up
'Cause like the old vet that strives for the cup
I'll never give up
I'll never give up

<u>ANNIVERSARY BLUES</u>

June twenty-eighth
The worst of days
I lost my faith
In so many ways

So much pain
In both body and mind
Nothing to gain
This life so unkind

It hits each year
Such sorrow and woe
The time that I fear
When my injury shows

This depression once lasted
For the longest duration
To know now it will pass
Is my sole consolation

BETWEEN TWO WORLDS

There exists such a conflict between body and mind
It's especially tough when these two worlds collide
At once I'm a child who pees in his bed
Who at times such as those wishes he was dead

Sometimes I'm so tired I just want to sleep
Yet I need to prepare so I don't spring a leak
There are the hours I need to get ready for work
To be sure I'm not late and feel like a jerk

At the same time in my head is a normal young man
Who believes he's equipped to do anything you can
To feel this allows me to function each day
Without it, for me, there is no other way

To split these two lives seems an impossible task
Indeed it's a goal of myself that I ask
It starts with acceptance for this to occur
A lifelong struggle to prevent such a blur

BARRIERS

There are so many barriers I face in my life
That can add to my everyday struggles and strife
And while it may be difficult to name them all
These are by far the easiest to recall

There's the inability to fit into the bathroom stall
The curb with no cut to enter the mall
The snow on the ground that has yet to be plowed
The elevator stuck, no way up, no way down

It is hard to predict just when they'll appear
These obstacles that are such a pain in the rear
Yet of all the barriers I face now and then
None is more daunting than not thinking I CAN!

FUTURE UNKNOWN

There's nothing so scary as a future unknown
To pray day and night though nothing is shown
The fear is so close, paralyzing and tight
You wonder if anything will ever go right

After all, is this really the best it will get?
With nothing to show but lost time and regret
And yes it may be the hardest to face
Not knowing the time, person or place

Yet what is the solution, does anyone know?
But to live day by day and work hard as you go
For that is the answer I've found works the best
And let time itself take care of the rest

<u>LUCKY</u>

I sit in the sun and feel the warm breeze
This is when I am the most at ease
Feeling all of life's tensions go slipping away
So that I can face another grueling day

Perspective is hard to come by most times
We get so caught up in our day to day lives
Sitting back and reflecting how far we have come
When many may have said it could never be done

Such moments of peace seem so far between
When I consider myself in nature's grand scheme
So it's times like these I consider with pride
How lucky I am to be alive

THANK YOU

Your son won't live you heard them say
They all agreed the injuries were too great
It's better to let him rest in peace
Doing much more won't help him now

When my eyes opened you exclaimed
Look what he did my boy is alive
The doctors in frenzy went to work
To get me the help they could not provide

Then you heard another sad line
His life will never amount to much
He'll never breathe without this machine
There's no doubt been damage to his brain

Still you held strong saying give him a chance
You never wavered though others did
There's something you saw in this pain stricken boy
Your insistence fevered with blind hope

How tired and drained you both must have been
Returning to battle each war stricken day
There you were through every hard moment
Comfort and strength melded to one

Recovery process so hard and so slow
Setbacks like minefields along the way
Progress was measured, celebrations in turn
Acknowledgements needed to continue the grind

Not that my life now is all great
I have limits still present from that fateful day

Keep On Pushing

They won't disappear no matter the effort
But with love and support my focus has changed

Despite what I do, without you I'm not here
With a life worth living and rewards all around
Thank you so much for pursuing that chance
We proved them all wrong, a team to the end

Derek Hawkins

PRIORITIES

Baseball games and TV shows so unimportant
Distracting completely from a world of woes
Worried obsessions about our appearance
Charity spent on a third pair of shoes

The cynic inside says take care of you
People getting fat as funds are misspent
Programs existing to better the rich
Those in need still going without

Still a tug exists and pulls at the heart
A sickly pup brought to attention
We don't want to see yet can't help but look
Through anger and pity the channel is turned

A helpless feeling that's so overwhelming
No one alone can save the world
Too many problems to be addressed
Confusion sets in, another day goes past

Responsibility maybe lies within
Focusing on what matters the most
Hoping to play my own small part
I acknowledge a power greater than mine

A PEACEFUL SLEEP

What if one day the sun doesn't shine?
And nary a star appears in the sky
Darkness ahead and all around
Fears of death come to light

Will I have done all I wanted?
Before this flame of life burns out
Looking ahead so much to do
Needing to deal with what's been done

Not knowing when or how it will happen
How on earth can one prepare?
One minute here the next one gone
Or will there be a hundred years

Reflection is hard amongst struggle and chaos
Taking the time to be as one
Hoping to have that one more day
Regrets like ghosts haunt the mind

Longevity may not be the key
But accomplishing much in a short time
Take more risks or play it straight?
Sometimes the dead are walking alive

And so I hope to die in peace
Taking solace in a life well led
Not dwelling on what might have been
Having done the best with what I had

HEIDI'S POEM

Heidi is the name of my wife
She brings great joy into my life
We've been together many years
My love for her brings joyful tears

For her, it was love at first sight
Despite my obvious lack of height
For my part, attraction had to grow
Experience with love for us both was low

Rushed into a couple before being friends
This would come to hurt in the end
It eventually led to us breaking up
Emptiness followed like a bone dry cup

Our months apart did the most good
Though at the time who thought it would
Our friendship grew and we got back together
A foundation laid down to stay forever

Events have tested our resolve
That served to help our relationship evolve
Me having gone away to school
Alone and frightened like an ant in a pool

Coming home for good felt so right
Engagement brought us such delight
Waiting impatiently for our day
Wanting it to come in the very worst way

And then the time was finally here
For all to dance, and laugh and cheer

Words will never begin to describe
How happy I was to take her as my bride

Marriage has brought such complete happiness
Something with which I never thought I'd be blessed
And so I promise to her it will be
Together forever, just her and me

DIVINE INTERVENTION?

I wonder how much things are meant to be
And to what extent this applies to me
Acceptance is easy, when things fall in my favor
These are the times to relish and savor

It's a comfort to know that things will work out
Through past experience I'm talking about
Providing strength in the end to overcome
Like learning to solve a tricky sum

I get into trouble when recalling my injury
The master plan remains a mystery
Could I have had all this without getting hurt?
Searching for answers, all of them curt

How could this be preordained?
Do we get to choose along the way?
Is there some other force beyond us in charge
That chooses our fate, by and large?

Maybe instead there's a compromise
I'll try that shoe on for size
Divine plans, like human ones, going awry
Who am I to wonder why?

'Why me?' does nothing but hold me back
Preventing a full on, aerial attack
It's easiest sometimes to say "shit happens"
Like a bird in flight, our wings must keep flappin'

<u>TIME AGAIN</u>

It's feeling like this time of year
The season I love, but day I hate
Nothing seems to go right
Cursing everything in sight

Mood swings ever more apparent
Reflections reveal a steely shine
Heaviness weighs down the air
Caught again in a blank-eyed stare

Everyday life gets much harder
Vision skewed to what I've lost
Surrounded by nothing but limits
The road ahead littered with divots

After so many years it still occurs
Though accomplishments seem to lessen the blow
A different person from year one to eighteen
One from the beginning I couldn't have seen

This harrowing mourning is essential
Not staying too long within the self
Careful to avoid lashing out
Coping effectively is what counts

Does time itself heal such wounds?
Or like cuts do they scab and itch
An annual event, no end seems near
It's feeling like this time of year

WITHOUT SPORT

As a child, playing sports was such a high
Being the goalie was my favorite
Stricken at 9 in the blink of an eye
Much too young to truly savor it

Competition was fierce among us kids
Status determined through wins and losses
On this being a privilege no one took bids
A nightmare was waiting with turns and tosses

The accident however wasn't a dream
From it there would be no waking up
A player was lost from the neighborhood team
Like a litter left with a damaged pup

Attempts were made to rejoin the crowd
Especially in games of baseball and hockey
The end result, me crying aloud
Things had changed so much it was shocking

Without athletics a void remains
Part of my being continuously suppressed
Searching for outlets that seldom contain
The concept of challenge that brings out my best

SEEING ME

Why is it so hard to see what I see
Somehow it's not revealed, what is inside of me
It is the chair alone that they think I'm about
Assumptions are made with no questions, no doubt

Yet I am a person who thinks just like them
Who knows that a diamond is also a gem
To prove this point is my sole desire
The goal to which I have long aspired

Sadly though it may never come true
Not everyone will view what's inside of you
To settle this conflict remains very hard
I gain an inch but then lose a yard

I wish I had power to rearrange
The thoughts of others I know I can't change
It all must come down to how I feel
The struggle inside to keep things real

ME AND 9/11

It must be a joke I thought to myself
The radio tuned to 'The Morning Show'
Driving to work on a Tuesday morning
As the story developed there was such a shock

How dare this be done to my homeland!
These United States of America
The land of the free, home of the brave
With freedoms given the ultimate protection

A personal connection didn't exist
Lives that were lost having no relation
Yet the impact simply could not be denied
A country in mourning, a nation in peril

The passing of time has allowed for reflection
Things taken for granted in our lives
So much we have exists no where else
Leading the way in so many advances

Would I've survived my accident if living abroad?
So urgently I was in need of care
From "simple" highways to complex medications
A new perspective on how I'm still alive

Realizations should not have to come from tragedy
Though this seems to be the way of the world
A weakness perhaps of human behavior
Not honoring that which is most important

PASSING JUDGEMENT

I was to be her very first love
Though I didn't think she was sent from above
A bit underweight with hair long and frizzy
Her love was enough to make us both dizzy

How ironic it was that I was the judge
While she was the one without a grudge
Accepting me solely for who I am
Seeing the chair but not giving a damn

I expected my scars would scare her away
Expecting to be left alone each day
Yet she remained, firm through it all
Refusing to walk, just standing tall

How ashamed I am, now looking back
That she was the one under attack
What an incredible beauty she has become
My heart now beats loud as a drum

My spitefulness almost didn't let it work
Man how I would have felt like a jerk
Living without her is hard to imagine
I'm glad for my sake that didn't happen

NOTHING SPECIAL

To some I have no intelligence at all
A head exists but houses no brain
It becomes so clear with that stupid look
Met with the tone that says 'poor guy'

And yet to others I am such a genius
All that shut in time conducive to study
Can do nothing else so I must be smart
I guess they think we're all Stephen Hawking

A few may meet these select criteria
As are likely to be when talking extremes
Most, like me, fall right in the middle
Just an average Joe with goals and a wife

Fortunately there are those who see just that
Who look at the eye and not the wheel
These are the ones I devote my time to
With positive influences on my life

Those with prejudices aren't worth changing
Being thankful they don't rule the world
Banging your head only ends in bleeding
Precious time wasted with no return

THE A TO Z OF DISABILITY

Anger, accessibility, aggravation, assumptions, anesthesia
Believing, bewildered, bending
Confusion, control, confidence, crazy
Disgust, disillusion, duress, desire, destruction, destiny
Everlasting, ego, emptiness, empowering
Forgiveness, fortitude, forever, fear, fairness, frustration
Growth, guilt, grieving
Humbling, hateful, hindering, humor
Insight, intelligence, introspection, impatience, incomplete, ignorance, independence
Jealousy, juvenile, justification, jolting
Killing, kindness, knowledge
Loathing, life, levity, liability, levelheaded
Militant, maneuvering, madness, millisecond
Never, notice, needing, nervousness
Overwhelming, overcome, open
Powerful, punitive, prisoner
Quiet, quitting, quality
Respect, reflection, restless, rational
Sensitive, stagnant, stereotype, stolen, spirit, support
Therapy, trauma, torment, tragedy, timid
Unspoken, unbelievable, unyielding
Victory, vindication, value, vengeance
Wishful, winter, whole, wondering, willful
Extreme, extend, exist
Youth, yesterday
Zero, zest

EMOTION'S VENGEANCE

A regular guy walks down the street
Someone you might want to meet
Yet no one ever gets to know
The pain inside that continues to grow

This guy keeps it all inside
Feelings he is prone to hide
He'll never cry on anyone's shoulder
With each passing day he becomes colder

It's never been his place to share
No one would understand or care
He'd rather go on being unhappy
At least he wouldn't be weak or sappy

And so he'll be strong while going gray
Misery growing with each day
Forever remaining private and stoic
Believing he's being downright heroic

Dealing in this way has its drawbacks
Soon this man will receive a payback
Like a teapot without a spout
He doesn't let the anger out

So he moves toward a final showdown
Will anyone ever get the lowdown?
The curtain will fall on a final scene
Taking his life may be the means

DEATH IN LIVING

Is to die an end?
To one day never be
Breath that won't come again
Not another thing to see

Blackness surrounds and blocks all light
Like the moon across our sun
Images fade from memory's sight
What is done is truly done

Reality cuts through like a knife
I will not live forever
Finite indeed is this life
Viewed as a curse and a treasure

We all live by what we leave
A stamp not easily erased
Good or bad, no matter the deed
A legacy left for all to face

Is death not an end but instead a process?
Ventured upon each waking day
One that ultimately could cost us
Choices mark what people will say

So life and death share this link
Separate terms they are no longer
A more optimistic way to think
My resolve to do better that much stronger

THE ROAD OF LIFE

Life is a road
Stretching far out of sight
In this body I drive
The most well oiled machine

The road ahead starts out real smooth
Pavement glides by with nary a crack
Full speed ahead in cruise control
Weather conditions ideal for travel

Moving along things become more uncertain
Like losing your way in the bad part of town
Potholes and divots crowd neglected streets
Detours and roadblocks with sights unfamiliar

In time there's a push through the other side
An on ramp appears to the main highway
Picking up speed on the road to freedom
Exits the fodder for enriching experience

Directions like choices come aplenty
Crises like accidents cause delays
Breaking the cycle of rubberneck traffic
The passage of time stuck in place

Soon the arrival of increased maintenance
Parts needing regular and careful inspection
A higher octane fuel is required
Ensuring performance in proportion with age

If fortune smiles an antique may result
Gaining its share of admiring stares
Retiring to drives in more tranquil circumstance
Shining example of what was and can be

THE MEMORY OF ME

Hello little boy from long ago
An echo growing faint and distant
How I long to see your smile
So bright and full of innocence

Tragedy came and struck so quick
Just like a thief in the night
You never even had a chance
All was stolen in an instant

The list of things to accomplish
The count is truly endless
You dreamed so much to become an athlete
I believe you could have done it

But then the pain came in waves
Both the mental and the physical
I see you now in my mind's eye
Powerless to protect you

I am so sorry for all you endured
You could never have deserved it
Blame is not yours to own
The fates were all against you

I honor you now by doing my best
So your death is not in vain
While I know it's not the same
It's my sole means of acceptance

With the passage of time you become less real
Both a blessing and a curse

At once it hurts to remember your skills
Yet it brings joy to know I wasn't always this way

And so we'll part till another time
When you're sure again to visit
I hope to see your smile one day
In the wide eyes of my own child

FREE OF STARES

I feel these stares all around me
Difficult to escape
Piercing eyes I find astounding
Looking as if I'm an ape

High school years spent alone
A friend not to be found
The ability to fit in was stolen
Feeling like a mole in the ground

A lost boy starving for attention
A young man without a home
To isolate was a common penchant
Waiting for the way to be shown

Hateful is this low self esteem
A closed throat leads to holding back
Thinking too much, unable to breathe
Confidence continues to lack

Yet rewards only follow from risk
Feeling discomfort and completely vulnerable
The option to be alone, as cold as the wind's brisk
Deep down no one wants to be miserable

Breaking through to the other side
There is no better feeling
To finally be free of a desire to hide
Stares no longer send me reeling

Derek Hawkins

BEAUTIFUL DAY

Bone chilling temps
Unmanageable snow
Piled up bills
Enduring wet jeans
Sinus pressure headache
On the job stress
Rain drenched clothes
Family dysfunction
That time of the year blues
A task forgotten
A restless night's sleep
An early wake up call
The cat acting bad
A still angry wife
Awareness of limits
Longing for change
Putting on a few pounds
Stuck indoors
Dying of boredom
An inaccessible bathroom
A pulled muscle
A bad bed sore

THROUGH YOUR EYES

Let me in is what you said
I want to know what's in your head
All that hurt you keep inside
Holding on to foolish pride

I look but then you turn away
Leave me alone is what you say
Tempting when you're in this mood
We both know will do no good

I wish you could see what I see
Then maybe you would be with me
Instead of putting up your walls
You'd respond favorably to my calls

You treat me with such resentment
Pretty soon I'll lose contentment
There's a better way I deserve to be treated
Your love and respect is what I've needed

Such bitterness in the end will destroy you
I hope that's a conclusion you can come to
What I've said proved to make no difference
In changes I have longed to witness

So now we've reached a boiling point
This relationship is out of joint
My gift of time has become impatience
Are you lost or can we go the distance?

<u>MY SURVIVAL</u>

To survive is to cope
To overcome through acceptance
What today can't be changed
And what tomorrow will remain

To survive is a mindset
To bend and not break
Holding on for dear life
Despite great adversity

To survive is to seek help
To not stand foolishly alone
Calling on support when needed
Taking no one for granted

To survive is to persist
To try that much harder
Striving toward improvement
Not resting on what's been

I am a survivor

HOME AGAIN

Here I am
Back again
In the hospital
My old friend

This is merely a visit
I'm glad to say
Like a vacation spot
I wouldn't want to live

How ironic it is
This feeling of comfort
So undesirable
Yet so hard to fight

Where my life once ended
Now life breathes in
The high inescapable
Better than drugs

The best part of all is I get to leave
Hop in my car and head for home
Having connected with my spirit
I am devoid of sadness

CPSIA information can be obtained at www.ICGtesting.com
Printed in the USA
LVOW071939020812

292739LV00001B/1/P